SAINT JEROME

SAINT JEROME

The Early Years

PAUL MONCEAUX

Translated by F. J. SHEED

CLUNY
Providence, Rhode Island

CLUNY EDITION, 2024

This Cluny edition is a republication of *St. Jerome: The Early Years*,
originally published in 1933 by Sheed & Ward.

For more information regarding this title
or any other Cluny Media publication,
please write to info@clunymedia.com, or to
Cluny Media, P.O. Box 1664, Providence, RI 02901

WWW.CLUNYMEDIA.COM

Cluny edition copyright © 2024 Cluny Media LLC

All rights reserved.

ISBN: 978-1685953492

NIHIL OBSTAT: Eduardus J. Mahoney, S.Th.D., *censor deputatus*

IMPRIMATUR: Joseph Butt, *Vic. Gen.*
WESTMONASTERII, DIE 20 JANUARII 1933

Cover design by Clarke & Clarke
Cover image: Antonello da Messina,
Saint Jerome in His Study,
c. 1475, oil on limewood
Courtesy of Wikimedia Commons

CONTENTS

	Preface	1
	Introduction	5

PART I: CHILDHOOD AND SCHOOLDAYS

I.	*Childhood*	15
II.	*At School in Rome*	24

PART II: FROM SCHOOL TO THE DESERT

	Introductory	47
I.	*Baptism*	49
II.	*Gaul and the Ascetic Vocation*	62
III.	*Aquileia*	68
IV.	*Departure for the East*	75
V.	*The Charms of Antioch*	84
VI.	*The Dream*	94
VII.	*Entry into the Desert*	102

PART III: THE DESERT

	Introductory	109
I.	*Jerome's Cave in the Desert*	111
II.	*Hymn to the Desert*	121
III.	*Letters from the Desert*	131
IV.	*The Life of St. Paul the Hermit*	142
V.	*The "Temptations" of St. Jerome*	155
VI.	*Warfare in the Desert*	163
VII.	*Farewell to the Desert*	173
VIII.	*Jerome at Thirty*	178

To
THE RIGHT REVEREND
IGNATIUS SYLVESTER MOONEY, O.S.B.,
ABBOT OF DOUAI

PREFACE

AMONG the Fathers of the Church there is no more original writer, none more individual, vivid, witty—amusing even—than St. Jerome. He is a born writer; fresh, sparkling with verve and malice, with bursts of satire and flashes of genius. He is an incomparable letter-writer, a pleasant storyteller, a biting and furious controversialist, a pamphleteer at need. He is also a great scholar—in Greek, Hebrew, exegesis, history—a sound critic apart from moments of partiality. Above all, he has a genius for translation—so great a genius that his Latin translation of the Bible, adopted officially by the Church, has become our Vulgate, and resounds each day throughout the Catholic world. Such literary achievements are somewhat above the average, even for a Saint and Father of the Church.

As a writer Jerome merits to be read and re-read by all concerned with the trade of letters and to be better known to the public. And he will be all the more enjoyed, as he is today—thanks to the labours of contemporary scholars—better comprehended.

PAUL MONCEAUX

Already in his lifetime he was greatly admired, and he rapidly became a kind of classic. He was much read in the Middle Ages—the clergy had made him their patron, and legend had made him a cardinal. By that time, artists delighted in painting the principal scenes of his life. To the Humanists of the Renaissance he was a passion—a master in the art of writing.

Since the seventeenth century his literary glory has rather gone into eclipse behind his aureole as a saint. For the greater part of the nineteenth century scholars and men of letters more or less neglected his work. Those who did speak of him were content to fall back on the older works, good in their time, of Tillemont or Vallarsi. There was no critical edition. A traditional chronology was accepted, lacking solid foundation and often making a wrong relation of his writings either with one another or with the circumstances of his life. Legends which were actually in contradiction with the character of the man were still half credited. And far too much unction was credited to this mighty fighting man. Even quite recently, in one place or another, he has figured either according to the edifying commentaries of Tillemont or according to the long-celebrated work of Amédée Thierry—a book which undoubtedly contains brilliant pictures, but of uncertain accuracy and now considerably out-of-date.

In short, the whole study of St. Jerome had to begin

SAINT JEROME: THE EARLY YEARS

again at the beginning. It has already made excellent progress. We now have critical editions of several of his works, notably of the *Letters*, by M. Hilberg in the *Corpus scriptorum ecclesiasticorum latinorum*, issued by the University of Vienne. Then various scholars have turned their attention to this or that part of the work; sometimes even to the whole. Apart from innumerable shorter articles, there is Goelzer's essay on St. Jerome's Latinity, Brochet's on St. Jerome and his enemies, the small biography by Largent in the *Collection des Saints*, the great monograph of Grützmacher, the *Miscellanea Geronimiana*, published in Rome for his fifteenth centenary, the little book by Dom Leclercq. Finally, most important of all, the first two volumes of the *Spicilegium sacrum Lovaniense* published by the University of Louvain, embody the results of M. Cavallera's immense effort of research upon the biography of St. Jerome and the chronology of his works.

Thanks to all these labours, we are today able to draw a more accurate picture of the Saint's life—his adventures, his relations, his works and his significance. Here I shall speak only of his youth, the account of which needed re-making. It seemed simplest to set it down as narrative, indicating as I went the points where correction had had to be made.

The principal source is the immense, infinitely rich and varied work of Jerome himself; very fortunately he loved talking of himself and his affairs. Upon this source I have

PAUL MONCEAUX

always drawn directly, not neglecting others, and using as need arose the results of contemporary scholarship.[1]

To the story of Jerome I have added descriptions of the more interesting among the works of art—some of them masterpieces—in which scenes of his life (the more picturesque especially) have been illustrated.[2]

It only remains for me to thank the eminent director of the *Revue des Deux Mondes*, who had much to do with the genesis of this book. While welcoming my idea of bringing together, for the reading public, the results of a long process of research, carried on over many years in the Collège de France, M. Doumic decided the form the work should take. Thus these studies on the youth of St. Jerome were first presented to the public, at least in part, in two articles in the *Revue* entitled: "St. Jerome in the Desert of Syria."[3]

---

1. I shall be excused, even perhaps thanked, for not unduly multiplying references. In general, apart from a few necessary exceptions, my principle has been to give textual references only for passages translated from Jerome's works. For other less indispensable references—the mass of which would have doubled the length of the book and smothered the book itself—readers should turn to the very complete tables at the end of M. Cavallera's fully documented monograph *Saint Jérôme, sa vie et son oeuvre*, 2 vols., 8 vo. (Louvain and Paris, 1922).
2. Many ancient pictures of which I shall have occasion to speak, representing scenes in the life of St. Jerome, are reproduced in M. Salomon Reinach's well-known collection *Répertoire de peintures du Moyen Age et de La Renaissance*, 6 vols., 16 mo. (Paris: Leroux, 1905–1923).
3. *Revue des Deux Mondes* (July 1 and 15, 1930).

INTRODUCTION

SAINT JEROME'S AGE

JEROME—in Latin *Eusebius Hieronymus*—was born about the year 347, in the town of Stridon, in the north-east corner of Italy.

These three lines summarise a great mass of research work. They contain two new facts, now apparently established, and of the utmost importance for Jerome's biography—the date of his birth, the geographical situation of his birthplace. Many contemporary scholars deserve to gain indulgences through the Saint's intercession, for they have cut about sixteen years off his age, thus destroying at their root the absurd legends as to the so-called decrepitude of the so-called centenarian.

For long it has been assumed on the word of Prosper of Aquitaine that Jerome was born in 331 and died in 420, which made him ninety. Hence the legends which picture him towards the end of his life as a broken old man. St. Augustine, who had never actually set eyes upon his correspondent and confrère in sanctity, thought him older than he was, and this fact has helped in the genesis of the legends:

for his distant friend was scarcely dead when we find him writing that Jerome "had lived on to decrepitude."[1] Certain biographers, outdoing Augustine and Prosper in generosity, have promoted Jerome to the dignity of a centenarian.

Upon this the imagination of artists has richly embroidered. They have actually gone one worse than the literary tradition, in that they have practically always confused his two sojourns in the East—his life in the desert and his life in the monastery at Bethlehem—thus making a composite picture of the young hermit and the old abbot. I may mention three examples. In the church of Santa Maria dei Frari at Venice there is a statue of St. Jerome by Alessandro Vittoria, a Venetian sculptor of the Renaissance. In this statue the Saint, holding in his right hand the stone of penance and in his left a book, is completely bald, fleshless, almost corpse-like in his rigidity—it is said to be a portrait of Titian at the age of ninety-eight. Now, the historical Jerome at the time of his hermitage in the desert was barely thirty. Turn now to the painting of St. Jerome by Ribera in the Museum of Naples, which looks so pitiful that irreverent critics have described it as a picture of an old beggar. And then there is the St. Jerome of Hennier: he is naked in the desert, flat on the ground, his hands clasped, looking so old and so dismal that he might very well be dead—he who at

---

1. *Contra Iulianum*, I, 34.

SAINT JEROME: THE EARLY YEARS

that moment was overflowing with life in the springtime of his thirty years.

These are but three examples chosen among a hundred, which bear witness down the centuries to the popularity of a legend born of a historical error. Turn back now to Prosper of Aquitaine, to show that he was wrong in this matter, as in a great many others.

Jerome himself provides us with our proof. The information he gives as to his family, his education, and various circumstances of his life, make it practically impossible that Prosper's statement as to the date of his birth should be correct. And, apart from anything else, it is impossible to harmonise the legend of a broken-down old man with the certain fact, attested by works still extant of which the date is known, of the astonishing polemical and literary activity displayed by him almost to the day of his death. It is unwise to argue from the passages where he speaks vaguely of his age; a man of vivid imagination, temperamental, often ill, he styles himself old or young according to the mood of the moment—sometimes both in the same work.

But there are precise facts which stand in absolute contradiction to the traditional chronology. Among these facts one is decisive. He tells us that the Emperor Julian's death (June 363) he was still a pupil in a grammarian's

---

2. *Comment. in Habacuc*, II, 3.

school.[2] Now according to the date of birth given by Prosper of Aquitaine, he would then have been thirty-two, which means that he might well have been the father of his classmates. We know that according to the normal cycle of studies, Roman boys entered the grammar school at twelve, leaving it at sixteen to follow the courses of rhetoricians, philosophers, or jurists, and we know that their scholastic education ended with their twentieth year. We possess proof that it was still so in the second half of the fourth century; for example, when Augustine left the grammarian's classes and returned from Madaura to Tagaste in 370 he was sixteen. We even possess the text of an official document, practically contemporary, which sets down the age limits rigorously. It is a law of the Emperor Valentinian promulgated on March 12, 370. It was directed at students coming from the provinces to Rome, and it forbade them to stay on in the capital beyond their twentieth year, that is beyond the time when their studies were completed.[3]

From the terms of this law, and from the fact of St. Augustine bidding farewell to grammar at sixteen, the conclusion obviously to be drawn is that Jerome, being still a pupil of the grammarians in June 363, was at that time not more than sixteen. This places the year of his birth at the earliest in 347. Probably that was the year, for there are

---

3. *Confess.* II, 2, 4; III, 5–6.

SAINT JEROME: THE EARLY YEARS

several arguments against making him younger still. This date fits ill with the legend, but is in harmony with every known circumstance of his life.

On the geographical position of Stridon, his birthplace, there has been vigorous discussion for centuries. On this matter tradition and legend have been complicated by the claims of nationality, claims in hopeless contradiction one with another. The controversy grew to a high point of bitterness during the nineteenth century, with the awakening and development in Central Europe of rival national feelings. Jerome himself, who is the only author of antiquity to mention Stridon, provides the ground of this battle whereof he is the trophy. He had written in 392 in his own biography: "Hieronymus, son of Eusebius, was born in the town of Stridon, which has since been destroyed by the Goths and which was formerly a *confinium* of Dalmatia and Pannonia."[4] This has practically always been translated: "On the borders of Dalmatia and Pannonia." From this mistranslation there has arisen a whole literature in many tongues, urging the claims of many nations.

Jerome and his glory have been tossed from side to side in the dispute. Scholars of divers countries, in divers languages, have affirmed that he was a Dalmatian or a Pannonian, from this or that canton of Pannonia or Dalmatia.

---

4. *De viris*, 135.

PAUL MONCEAUX

Claims have been put in on behalf of Austria, Hungary, Bosnia, and Istria. They have even tried to make a Slav of him. Of recent years the attempt has often been made to place Stridon at Grahovo in Bosnia: there was much talk of an alleged inscription said to have been seen there, which they say marked the limit of the territory of the *Stridonenses*. But the inscription has disappeared and is known only by a shapeless unintelligible copy, a mere scrawl, in which nothing can be distinguished save by the eyes of faith. The other hypotheses are of no more importance. They all rest upon nothing; all betray considerations which have nothing to do with historical science. All their advocates may be dismissed as special pleaders.

The truth is that for anyone reasonably acquainted with the Latin of the late fourth century the word *confinium* is sufficient of itself to indicate the solution. The word had at that time a precise technical meaning, as Du Cange has shown, a meaning which had already begun to take shape in certain passages in the classics. It meant a *neck* of land or territory, thrust between the frontiers of two domains or two countries. Now take a historical map of the Roman Empire of the fourth century and look at the northeast extremity of Italy. You will see that there, not far from Aquileia, at the foot of the Julian Alps, an outlying part of the province of Venetia-Histria—previously the Tenth Region of Italy—juts like a wedge between Roman Dalmatia and

SAINT JEROME: THE EARLY YEARS

Pannonia. That is the *Dalmatia Pannoniaque confinium* of which St. Jerome speaks. There obviously was situated the town of Stridon, the town of his birth. Jerome therefore was, quite simply, an Italian from the region of Aquileia. Many scholars had suspected it from his style, which certainly shows no mark either of the Dalmatian or the Pannonian.

In these two facts—the situation of his birthplace and the date of his birth—we have the first two landmarks, formerly lacking, for an exact biography of Jerome. It will be seen that they harmonise perfectly with all the known facts of his life, and that in a narrative built upon these foundations legends vanish of themselves, to yield place to the reality of history.

PART I

CHILDHOOD AND SCHOOLDAYS

CHAPTER I

CHILDHOOD

In the Museum of Bourg-en-Bresse, there is a pleasant picture, part of a triptych painted in grey with some touches of colour. A rich middle-class home in Stridon: a handsome bedroom elegantly furnished, in good taste; in the background, on the right, a great bed on which the mother is lying. In the foreground, in front of the bed, the nurse sits on a cushion holding the new-born Jerome in her arms. On the left, near the bed, in various attitudes, are three women carrying a variety of articles; beyond, a door through which are coming a man and a woman—relations or visitors.

This triptych, dated 1518, which has often been attributed to Wohlgemuth, is almost certainly a work of the old French school. The unknown artist, a man of talent, must have been guided in his work by some humanist familiar with the life of St. Jerome. The furniture, of course, the costume, the detail, bear the mark of the Renaissance. But in this artistic transformation of the scene there is nothing historically absurd. It was indeed in some such surroundings, in a family of that class, that Jerome was born.

PAUL MONCEAUX

He belonged to the comfortable middle-class of Stridon, that rich and important bourgeoisie which in all the Roman cities of the empire constituted a kind of provincial aristocracy. Judging by the look of the names borne by Jerome and his father, the family must have been Greek in origin. Probably it was descended from some farmer or shopkeeper who had come from the East to settle in this lost corner of Italy. Apart from the names, the family had become completely Latinised. It no longer spoke Greek, and to the younger brother of Jerome had been given the sound Latin name of Paulinianus. The family had prospered; it possessed considerable property in the district, lands and farms. More favoured by fortune than Augustine, Jerome had not to take up a trade for a living. When he received his inheritance from his parents he sold part of it to build his monastery at Bethlehem; later, still in the interests of his monastery, he sent his brother back home to sell up what farms and other real property still belonged to him.

With regard to his parents Jerome is surprisingly reticent. He tells us that his father was named Eusebius, and that is all. His mother he does not even name. Yet his parents were still alive in 374, when, at the age of twenty-seven, he set out for the East. Both must have been dead when he returned in 382. They were buried at Stridon on one of their properties—we find Jerome excusing himself in 398 for being forced to sell "the ashes of his parents" with his

SAINT JEROME: THE EARLY YEARS

farms.[1] We need not dwell on this unpleasing detail. But in a man so expansive we may well wonder whence came this repugnance to speak of his father and mother. The reason is that Jerome's letter-writing begins only in 374, with the beginning of his first sojourn in the East. Now, at this time he had already quarrelled with his parents over his ascetic vocation. If he had spoken of them at all, he would have had to pronounce severe judgment upon their attitude. He preferred to say nothing.

In compensation he retained a tender memory of a grandmother whose caresses and kindnesses he had enjoyed. Very often, he says, he had had to be torn from his grandmother's arms, to be dragged off to school, where the rod of an Orbilius awaited him.[2] He had also an aunt, Castorina, his mother's sister—a formidable aunt, who later on was to imagine that she had grievances against him; she did not answer his letters, and he wrote her again from the depths of his desert in the hope of winning her round.[3]

He was the eldest of three children. He had a sister and brother much younger than himself. His sister, whose name is unknown to us, was born about 360; she appears at first to have had worldly tastes, frivolous occupations, but little by little she came under the ascendancy of her

---

1. *Epist.* 66, 14.
2. *Apologia contra Rufinum*, I, 30.
3. *Epist.* 13.

elder brother. After some wavering and changes of mind, she finally vowed herself to asceticism under the spiritual direction of Julianus, deacon of Aquileia.[4] Probably it was this second conversion in the one family that led to the definitive breach with his parents. The younger brother, Paulinianus, was still a child in 374 when Jerome set out for the East—born at the earliest in 364, he was then barely ten. Yet he was to set his foot upon the same path. Later he joined Jerome in Rome. He embarked with him in August 385, and under his direction was monk and priest at the monastery of Bethlehem.

Thus all three children had been conquered in turn by the new asceticism. The elder brother was hermit, priest and monk, then abbot; the younger was likewise monk and priest; the sister was a nun or consecrated virgin. From all this we might be led to assume that there was an atmosphere of ardent devotion in the home. We have every reason to think that it was not so. If the eldest became a saint, his parents had nothing to do with it.

"I was born a Christian, of Christian parents," said Jerome one day.[5] Another time he wrote to the Patriarch of Alexandria: "From my cradle, so to speak, I have been nourished with Catholic milk."[6] His parents, then, were

---

4. *Epist.* 6 and 7.
5. Preface to the translation of Job from the Hebrew.
6. *Epist.* 82, 2.

SAINT JEROME: THE EARLY YEARS

Catholics, but it is pretty obvious that their faith was not particularly active. Such, in any case, was the prevailing spiritual state in the Christian community of Stridon. This we learn from Jerome, who has little tenderness for his compatriots. From the desert he wrote to friends at Aquileia: "My country is slave to ignorance—*rusticitatis vernacula*. For God they have their belly; they live from day to day; the richest is the holiest." And with regard to Lupicinus, the bishop of the place, the pious solitary added: "As the popular proverb has it, 'The lid matches the pot.'" In the same sense he applies the phrase which, according to Lucilius, once made Crassus laugh, the only time in his life: "To every mouth its own lettuce"—a phrase used of an ass eating thistles. The portrait of the bishop was completed by a cascade of proverbs: "He is a sick pilot steering a sinking ship, a blind man leading the blind into the ditch, a guide worthy of those he guides."[7]

Here you have the opinion of a holy man—not very patient, it is true, and given to resentment—concerning the Christians of Stridon and their bishop. There is, therefore, nothing surprising in the discovery that his parents were somewhat lukewarm Catholics, mainly concerned with worldly things. Certainly they had no understanding of the vocation of their children.

---

7. *Epist.* 7, 5.

On the other hand, they did not neglect the education of their eldest son, upon whose precocious intelligence the family built great hopes. For the moment it was a matter only of the most elementary instruction. Like the boy Augustine at Tagaste, the boy Jerome was sent to Stridon to one of those primary schools conducted by a *litterator* or *primus magister*. There he learned to read, write and figure. He joined in those infant groups which repeated *ad nauseam*: "One and one are two, two and two are four"—and like Augustine he probably added in a grim whisper: "Oh, the loathsome sing-song!"[8] Jerome, too, in spite of his intelligence and his taste for study, was often enough inattentive. His harmless distractions had certain disagreeable consequences. "We also," he wrote later, "learnt our letters; we also often drew back our hand to avoid the rod."[9] Instinctively he sought protection. That is why when school hour approached he was found in the arms of his grandmother.

He had at that time a special friend, Bonosus, who remained the closest friend of his youth. They were both from Stridon, and were the same age. They belonged to the same class, and their families were in close connection. They were brought up together. They had, we are told,[10] the same nurses and the same pedagogues, the same pleasures,

---

8. *Confess.* I, 13.
9. *Epist.* 50, 5.
10. *Epist.* 3, 4–5.

SAINT JEROME: THE EARLY YEARS

and the same small troubles. They began their studies together at Stridon, continued and completed them at Rome. They were baptized on the same day. They journeyed together to Gaul, stopping at the same inns, sharing the same meals. They took their vows of asceticism at the same time and began the ascetical life together in their retreat at Aquileia. They only parted at the age of twenty-seven to follow parallel ways in different solitudes. Bonosus became a hermit on a rock in the Adriatic, while Jerome went off to live as an anchorite in the desert of Syria. They owed to each other the two most precious conquests of their moral life: certainty of salvation by the way of asceticism, and initiation in friendship.

The years passed and the learning of the *litterator* of Stridon began to wear a little thin. Jerome tells us that he had "broken himself to the study of Latin almost from the cradle, among grammarians."[11] From this it follows that towards the end of his childhood in Stridon he had begun to attend a grammar school. Such schools there were in most of the cities of the Roman Empire. Usually they were in quite a small way. In Africa they were often established in mere sheds directly on the street, with great curtains covering the entry and preventing the passers-by from gazing in.[12] At Stridon, where the climate was more rigorous, they

---

11. Preface *to Job*.

could scarcely have found curtains sufficient, but the instruction given must have been roughly the same. In these small towns the master limited his ambition to some slight development of the primary education, to knocking the corners off children whom their families were shortly to send into the large cities in pursuit of more serious studies. Thus Jerome would not have felt altogether out of his element the day when at Rome he entered the school of Donatus.

Before following him into school, let us look for a moment at the schoolboy. He was then, as he was always to be, thin, highly strung, delicate in health. "My poor body is weak even when it is well," said Jerome later,[13] which did not prevent him from living to old age. The truth is that he had great energy, resilience, and strength of will. Headstrong and tenacious, he was throughout his life a persistent worker. As a child, he loved play as much as study; on holidays he enjoyed himself, playing hide-and-seek, he tells us, in the "cells of the slaves."[14] His minor sin seems to have been gluttony. He admits that at the time of his conversion to asceticism the sacrifice he found hardest to make was the sacrifice of good living.[15]

Delicate health, liveliness of mind as of body, passion

---

12. Augustine, *Confess.* I, 13.
13. *Epist.* 3, 1.
14. *Apologia contra Rufinum*, I, 30.
15. *Epist.* 22, 30.

SAINT JEROME: THE EARLY YEARS

for study and for games and for cakes, measureless ardour in friendship and already perhaps in enmity, such was Jerome at the age of twelve. In a word, he was like a great many children who never become great writers, nor scholars, nor saints.

CHAPTER II

AT SCHOOL IN ROME

JEROME was some twelve years old when he came to Rome with Bonosus in or about the year 359 to continue his studies. There he was to pass his boyhood and youth up to the age of twenty. We have no information as to his lodgment during that time; we may assume that he followed the usual custom and lived in the family of a friend or with some schoolmaster.

For four years he pursued the courses of a grammar school—a sort of college, roughly comparable to the French lycée or the English secondary school, but without their upper forms. There is an interesting picture of Jerome at school, shown on a panel of that same triptych of Bourg-en-Bresse which contains the picture of his birth. A classroom: in the background, on the right, under a window, a high desk loaded with books. In front of the desk, a group of six schoolboys sitting in various attitudes. In the foreground, on the right, stands Jerome, reading a book which he is holding in both hands. Facing Jerome, on the left, the master sitting in a kind of high chair. Behind the master,

SAINT JEROME: THE EARLY YEARS

two people standing. In front of the chair, a dog, asleep.

As in the other picture, apart from certain details—of furniture and such like—which betray the Renaissance, the general atmosphere of the thing is right; though we may wonder if Donatus would have allowed a dog in his classroom. For the master shown in the picture is probably the celebrated Donatus, grammarian and rhetorician, whose teaching was so much esteemed and whose influence was supreme in the world of school up to the Middle Ages. In fact Donatus was a man of very unusual ability, as we may judge from several of his works which have come down to us, more or less complete, though more or less worked over by later hands—two grammars, one elementary, the other more scholarly, with two valuable commentaries, on Terence and on Virgil. Jerome, therefore, was in good hands. If he drew great profit from the master's lessons, if later he made good use of them in his own works, he was not ungrateful. He misses no chance of saying that he was a pupil of the great Donatus, of declaring the measureless gratitude in which he holds him, of styling him his "master."[1]

We know pretty well the programme of the grammar school at that day. The pupils recited lessons for the strengthening and furnishing of their memory, they learnt by heart fragments of the Greek and Latin classics,

---

1. Such as *Chron. (ad ann.* 353), where he calls Donatus *praeceptor meus.*

PAUL MONCEAUX

especially Virgil. The master would read aloud a few pages of an author, usually a poet; then he had the same passage read by a pupil, correcting the pronunciation and improving the diction. From that they passed to a commentary on the text, which was examined from many angles, and made the subject of remarks of every kind—bearing on rules of grammar, prosody or metre, history, geography, literary or moral significance. The most important, and often the most formidable, exercise was the correction of written tasks—imaginary speeches put into the mouth of historical characters, prose paraphrases of some poetic episode, verse compositions on a set theme. Each in turn read out his exercise, while his classmates looked on enviously or ironically as the case might be. This practice was calculated to put a boy on his mettle and in some cases brought to light a real talent.

The grammarian taught also the elements of the sciences. There were periods for music. Take a copy of Virgil and the principal classics; add a Latin and a Greek-Latin dictionary, some outlines of history, ethics, mythology, metre, and you have something like the library of the average schoolboy of the fourth century.

What Jerome has to say of his schooldays enables us to know certain points definitely. We have, for instance, a list of the principal authors studied by him under Donatus and later quoted without any failure of memory: first of all Virgil; then Cicero, Sallust, Horace, Livy, Seneca, Pliny,

SAINT JEROME: THE EARLY YEARS

Quintilian, Fronto; Plautus, Terence and other writers of comedy; Persius and Juvenal. Supplementing the oral explanations of the master, the pupils have at their disposal a series of written commentaries: there was Donatus himself on Virgil and Terence; then there were Asper on Sallust and Virgil; Volcatius on Cicero's Orations; Victorinus on Cicero's Dialogues, and many others on Plautus, Lucretius, Horace, Persius and Lucan.

If the programme of work was more or less the same everywhere, yet each master had naturally his own individual method. Donatus' method we can gather from such of his commentaries as remain on Terence and Virgil—an attractive mingling of grammatical comments, literature, moral lessons, anecdotes and jests. Donatus had no superstitious respect for tradition, as we know from a phrase of his (apropos of a line of Terence) quoted for us by Jerome: "Devil take those who have already said what we had to say ourselves!"[2]

Greek held a comparatively small place in the schools of the fourth century. In this matter a few generations had seen a marked change. It was a far cry to the time when Rome seemed half-Greek; when Plautus, Terence, Lucretius, Catullus, could show their originality by translating the Greeks, when the imagination of Virgil and Horace was

---

2. *Comment. on Ecclesiastes* (Migne's *PL* 33:1071).

haunted by Homer and Pindar, when an emperor like Marcus Aurelius wrote his intimate thoughts in Greek, when Greek was spoken at the court of the Severi. Little by little—with accelerated pace after the foundation of Constantinople—the West had grown away from the East. From now on the majority of Latin writers, Augustine included, had small knowledge of the language of Plato, or even Plutarch. Jerome, at the time of his setting out for Antioch, was scarcely better equipped. His old-time friend, Rufinus, was later to say of him in controversy: "Before his conversion to the ascetical life he was, like me, completely ignorant of Greek literature and the Greek language."[3] Rufinus, of course, may well have been overstating the case in the interests of controversy. At Rome Jerome and he had learnt at least the elements of Greek; as proof, notice that both of them were able to follow lectures in Greek immediately upon their arrival.

In the summer of 363, Jerome was finishing his grammar school course, when news came of the death of the Emperor Julian, stricken down suddenly in the midst of his victorious campaign against the Persians. The persecution was at its height, so that we may imagine there was not much shedding of Christian tears over the Apostate. At the time, the boy heard a pagan make an odd remark: "How

---

3.   *Apologia contra Hieronymum*, II, 7.

SAINT JEROME: THE EARLY YEARS

can Christians assert that their God is patient and without hate? Naught could be more terrible or more swift than the outbursts of his wrath: not an instant could he delay his vengeance." The pagan was apparently jesting. But Jerome is not jesting when he adds that "the Church of Christ chanted with enthusiasm" a hymn of victory.[4]

For all that, the change of ruler concerned the boy less than his approaching change of school. He was about to leave the stool of the grammar-school pupil to stand before the throne of the rhetoricians. He had wit enough to understand that he owed much to the master he was leaving. Quite apart from all that he had learnt of grammar and literature, under Donatus he had acquired the sense of style. He had come to know that "in style, the brush that erases is of more use than the pen point that writes."[5] And, in listening to Donatus, in reading the satirists and the comedians, a sharp edge had come to that cutting wit, of which one day he made confession: "Of me also, one may say with Horace: 'He has hay on his horn.'"[6]

Now behold him, in the autumn of 363, a student of the rhetoricians. To begin with, he rather lost his bearings in this new world of young men intoxicated with liberty

---

4. *Comment. in Habacuc*, II, 3.
5. *Epist.* 50, 1.
6. *Epist.* 50, 5. (The reference is to the custom of binding with hay the horns of dangerous cattle.)

(with licence and disorder, too), grouped in powerful societies aimed as much at pleasure as at study. We know the vivid complaints of Augustine as to the brutality of the students at Carthage—at least of one set of them whose pleasure it was to smash up everything, who ruled by terror and made the lives of newcomers a torment. They called themselves *Eversores*, smashers. Augustine, sixteen, when he came there from Tagaste, was more than a little alarmed at their ways; but, already a diplomat, he thought it wise to humour his uproarious companions. He analyses subtly his state of mind at the time: "I lived among them with an impudent shame that I was not like them. I lived, therefore, with them, sometimes enjoying their friendship, always revolted by their actions."[7]

Some years later he returned to Carthage, this time as a teacher, so that he saw the same things from a new point of view. He found the *Eversores* pouring uproariously into the lecture-rooms, right up to his very feet. From that time he scourged their activities with uncompromising rigour. "They rush impudently into the class-rooms, looking almost like maniacs; they upset the order established by the master for the progress of his students. They commit every sort of misdeed with incredible foolishness—misdeeds which the laws would punish were they not protected by

---

7. *Confess.* III, 3, 6.

SAINT JEROME: THE EARLY YEARS

custom.... Such ways I had been loath to adopt as a student; now that I was teaching, I was forced to tolerate them in others."[8] They were the manners of savages; and exasperated by them, he suddenly threw up his work at Carthage and went to try his fortune in Rome—where the young were held to be better mannered.

Better mannered they were; but less honest. They never entered a class-room without the master's permission, but they had a way of slipping off when the time came for the payment of fees.

On his arrival at Rome Augustine, reckoning to live on his profession as rhetorician, opened a class. Men in the same line warned him of what was in store: "Here," he was told, "young men agree among themselves not to pay their master the agreed price. They suddenly go off to another master, false to their word, sacrificing justice to the love of money."[9] How correct was the warning, Augustine soon learnt to his cost. He tells us so in his *Confessions*, with an indication of exactly what he thinks of those admirable youths.

If these students were so loath to part with their money—money given them for their studies—it was because the pleasures they loved were plentiful in Rome and

---

8. *Confess.* V, 8, 14.
9. *Confess.* V, 12, 22.

had to be paid for. The theatre was a special attraction, and beyond that even was the circus, the amphitheatre. An incident has come down to us from the life of Alypius, the future Bishop of Tagaste. During his student days at Carthage, he had been won from his overwhelming passion for the games in the course of a lecture by Augustine, who, without in the least having Alypius in his mind, had commented with biting irony on pleasure of that kind. Later on, at Rome, where he was studying law, he let himself be taken along by companions in the direction of the amphitheatre, where gladiatorial contests were being held. They hustled him in. He protested, swore that he would keep his eyes shut till the contest was over. But he had not sworn to keep his ears shut. Suddenly the whole amphitheatre burst into storms of cheering. Curiosity won. Instinctively he half-opened one eye. In an instant the poor fellow was once more in the grip of his passion. Till the end of the games, he could not tear his eyes from the murderous spectacle, savouring it more than his companions.[10]

Even within the walls of their schools, the Roman students found expression for their *joie de vivre*. The colonnades rang with their erotic songs, songs inspired, as Jerome tells us,[11] by those Milesian tales so much in vogue

---

10. *Confess.* VI, 7, 8.
11. *Apologia contra Rufinum*, I, 17: "*Cirratorum turba Milesiarum in scholis figmenta decantet.*"

SAINT JEROME: THE EARLY YEARS

for so many centuries, so rich a mine for La Fontaine as for Petronius and Apuleius before him. In the schools of the capital there passed from mouth to mouth also jokes on a larger scale, which never failed to win the uproarious laughter of the young. We possess a specimen, one as it happens spoken of by Jerome, a piece of buffoonery called "The Little Pig's Will," the Testament of Grunnius Corocotta.[12] It is a parody of a legal document, the pig bequeathing the different parts of his body to his relations and friends. This absurdity could always rouse the students to mirth, "set their limbs shaking with the laughter of savages."[13]

Jerome never forgot the Grunnius Corocotta of his student days. Forty years later it came to his mind at Bethlehem, for it is under the sobriquet of "Grunnius" that Rufinus—once his friend, but now his *bête noire*—is made to bear the lashes of his sarcasm.

The students found so much pleasure bound up with their schools at Rome that many of them wanted to stay on in the capital when their studies were over. The government had to issue strict regulations to force them to leave. We have an official document of Jerome's time bearing on the matter—the law of the emperors Valentinian, Valens

---

12. *"Testamentum Grunnii Corocottae Porcelli decantant in scholis puerorum agmina eachinnantium"* (*Comment. in Esaiam*, XII, Praefat). The document has been published, edited by Bücheier (Berlin, 1912).

13. *Testamentum suis Bessorum cachinno membra concutiat* (*Apologia contra Rufinum*, I, 17). The Bessi were barbarians of Thrace.

PAUL MONCEAUX

and Gratian, addressed from Treves to Olybrius, prefect of Rome, March 12, 370. The principal articles of this regulation, issued with imperial authority, cast a strong light on the schools where Jerome was then studying.

Every young man who wished to go to Rome for purposes of study—either for the whole of his studies or their completion—must approach the governor of his province and obtain from him a passport, authorising him to go to the capital and setting forth his place of birth, family condition, titles, and qualifications. On arrival at Rome, the student must introduce himself to the *magister census* and present his passport. At the same time he must specify the kind of studies he intended to pursue and give his exact address in Rome. Thereafter he was placed expressly under police surveillance. They had to see that he followed faithfully the programme indicated; that his bearing in public was irreproachable and his reputation good; that he did not join dubious associations, go too often to the games, keep bad company or take part in over-lengthy feastings. If he contravened the regulation, he was liable to be beaten with rods publicly and packed off home. Serious students, youths who gave themselves conscientiously to the prescribed studies, might remain in Rome till their twentieth year. Once that time was up, those who did not of their own motion return, were to be taken into the custody of the prefect of the city and sent home. To ensure the rigid

SAINT JEROME: THE EARLY YEARS

enforcement of the regulation, the law concluded with a provision that the registration office, *officium censuale*, should draw up each month two lists of students—one, a list of newcomers showing their place of origin, the other of veterans who had reached the age-limit and "were to be sent back to Africa or the other provinces."[14]

Though such a notion must have been far enough from his mind, whoever drew up this official document has drawn a very interesting picture of the Roman schools of the day. It emerges pretty clearly that in the student world pleasure held no less a place, or rather a higher place, than work. Yet there were many very diligent students, notable among them Jerome. He took his share generously of the pleasures that were going, but he was the wonder of all by his persistent application to work, the quickness of his intelligence, his eloquence and his scholastic success. He was the soul of a little band of serious students, his chosen companions, who later, with one exception, were to remain his faithful friends. In this group were first, three of his compatriots, all of them from the region of Aquileia: Bonosus of Stridon, his boyhood friend, who later became a hermit; Rufinus of Concordia, mysterious and inaccessible in his precocious gravity, later a monk, an unwearying—and unreliable—translator; Heliodorus of Altinum, a most

---

14. *Cod. Theod.* XIV, 9, 1.

devoted friend, with plenty of good sense and intelligence, later bishop of the town of his birth.

This group of three was joined, among others, by a student who belonged to the highest aristocracy of Rome, and was the correspondent of Augustine and Paulinus of Nola. Jerome calls him his "fellow pupil, comrade, friend."[15] This was Pammachius. He became a senator and married Paula's daughter Paulina; after her death he became a monk, and at Ostia, in a hospice built at his own expense, laboured in the service of the broken and destitute.

Let us now follow the youths into the schools of the rhetoricians. Who their particular masters were we do not know. Jerome refers to them often, but never by name. It has been many times repeated that he was a pupil of Marius Victorinus, the famous African rhetorician. In the middle of the fourth century he was *the* rhetor of the moment at Rome. He was held to be a great man, the outstanding Latin orator and philosopher of the time. A statue of him was set up in the Forum of Trajan actually during his lifetime. There was exaggeration in all this, yet he was an eminent master. We have two groups of interesting books by him, one pagan, one Christian. To his pagan days belong a small book of rhetoric and logic on the *Definitions*, a commentary on Cicero's *De Inventione*, a treatise on metric and

---

15. *Epist.* 48, 1.

SAINT JEROME: THE EARLY YEARS

grammar. Among works by him totally lost and surviving only in fragments, some have played an important part in the history of philosophy—notably his translation of the *Categories* and the *Interpretation* of Aristotle, Porphyry's *Isagoge* and other neo-Platonist books. At that period, Victorinus waged ardent warfare against Christianity, pouring ridicule, even in his lectures and his commentaries, upon the dogmas of the Incarnation and the Resurrection.

Then, suddenly, he was converted; on the day of his baptism he made public retractation of his errors. His conversion caused a sensation: it contributed in some measure to the conversion of Augustine, and it is the subject of some of the most beautiful pages in the *Confessions*.[16] From the moment of his conversion, Victorinus became a champion of the Church. To this second period belong several treatises against the Arians, three commentaries on St. Paul's epistles, and finally three *Hymns* on the Trinity, very curious and beautiful prose-poems, constructed according to the laws of scriptural parallelism with strophes and chorus. In the adaptation to Christian use of neo-Platonism and the vocabulary of metaphysics, Victorinus showed the way to Augustine. In the technical language of logic, of which he was the real creator in Latin, he was the master of Boethius and indirectly of the whole Middle Ages.

---

16. *Confess.* VIII, 2, 3ff.

Such is the great rhetorician, grammarian, exegete, philosopher and controversialist who, we are asked to believe, succeeded Donatus as Jerome's master. But attractive as the theory is at first sight, it can scarcely be true. Certainly, Jerome knew Victorinus in Rome, heard him and admired him greatly. But, often as he speaks of him, he never calls him his master. In 363, when Jerome was beginning his study of rhetoric, Victorinus was no longer teaching. The year before, the famous edict of Julian forbidding Christians to teach literature and rhetoric had forced him to choose between his profession and his religion. He had not hesitated. Abandoning his school, he devoted himself to controversy and to scripture criticism. Therefore, strictly speaking, he now had no pupils.

But there was no shortage of rhetoricians in Rome. Jerome found other masters to initiate him in the mysteries of the art, and he practised eloquence before them with impassioned ardour. Later he loved to recall this stage of his education, the observations gathered, the authors studied and commented upon. He evoked memories of his vanished school-days, his emotions, the successes he had had, his triumphant "declamations in imaginary controversies."[17] They still haunted his imagination. Thirty years after, in his monastery at Bethlehem, he dreamt by night

---

17. *Epist.* 81, 3.

SAINT JEROME: THE EARLY YEARS

of the excitements and the triumphs of his student days, living them again to the point of nightmare: "Now when my hair is white and baldness is upon me, often I see myself in a dream, curly-headed and wearing the toga, declaiming some small controversial matter before the rhetorician. I wake, overjoyed to have escaped the ordeal of this rhetorical exercise."[18]

In his free time Jerome loved to go to the lectures at the Athenaeum. This was a public establishment of general education, founded in Rome by the Emperor Hadrian for the advancement of letters and science, roughly on the lines of the Athenaea, which for long had existed in many Greek towns in the precincts of temples of Athene. Once when Jerome and Pammachius were at this Roman Athenaeum, the speaker quoted the phrase of Cato: *Sat cito, si sat bene* (It is quick enough if it is good enough). The phrase had a surprising reception: the crowd roared with laughter, presumably at the cacophony. All over the room students were shouting in chorus: *Sat cito, si sat bene!* Jerome admits that he shouted and laughed with the rest.[19]

As was customary, he listened to real speakers, speakers on real matters, by way of complement to the instruction of the rhetoricians. He attended the sittings of the courts, to

---

18. *Apologia contra Rufinum*, I, 30.
19. *Epist.* 66, 9.

hear the best-known advocates; and was astonished to hear them quarrelling in public like street-porters. "When I was a young man declaiming controversies at Rome, preparing for real contests by imaginary pleadings, I went much to the law courts. I saw the most eloquent of the orators arguing among themselves with extraordinary animosity. Often, leaving aside the matter under discussion, they took to personal insults, mocking and sneering at one another furiously."[20] These perhaps were the best lessons in controversy that Jerome was ever to have.

Back in his lodgings, he copied manuscripts. Books were his passion. But books were terribly expensive, and a student's budget, even if he were tolerably well-off, was hard to square with the demands of the booksellers. Many students were reduced to making copies, borrowing the book and transcribing the whole of it by hand. This Jerome did, with splendid tenacity, and so built up for himself a precious library of the classics, from which he could never bear to be parted. He took it with him later in his travels over the world, even to the East. "I could not now do without the library I had made for myself at Rome with unflagging labour."[21] Invariably, in every country to which destiny was to take him he made additions to his library.

---

20. *Comment. in Epist. ad Galatas*, I, 2.
21. *Epist.* 22, 30.

SAINT JEROME: THE EARLY YEARS

During his stay in Gaul, at Treves, he transcribed Christian works. At Antioch he trained copyists and took them with him to the desert itself. At Jerusalem he set the monks of the Mount of Olives toiling for him. At Caesarea he procured the works of Origen. At Bethlehem he organised from among his monks a band of copyists. At the end he had at hand in his monastery one of the richest libraries of the day, wherein Christian authors rubbed shoulders with the classics, Latin with Greek and Hebrew. This library of his was probably the thing he valued most in the world. Of all his ruling passions, its enrichment was perhaps the most constant and tenacious.

And the miniaturists of the Middle Ages realised it. In the Bibles and liturgical books in which St. Jerome is so often depicted, he is shown no less often as a bibliophile than as a translator or commentator. To take a single example, a miniature in the famous *Book of Prayers* of Charles the Bald, Jerome is copying a manuscript. He is seated, wearing a long robe; his left hand is resting on the volume, in his right he holds a pen, dipping its end in the ink. Costume apart, it is the real historical Jerome; the Jerome of the desert and Bethlehem, as much as the Jerome of Gaul or Rome.

While continuing his studies with the rhetoricians, Jerome was following courses in philosophy. He was interested particularly in ethics, principally the ethics of the Stoics, and in logic. Among the books of logic he was then working at he mentions the *Categories*, the *Interpretation* and the *Analitica* of Aristotle, Cicero's *Topica*, the *Commentary* upon Aristotle by Alexander of Aphrodisias, the *Isagoge* of Porphyry—probably in Victorinus' translation.[22] It was during these last student years that he got together all the philosophical knowledge he was ever to have. Long after—in his controversies with Rufinus—he made mention of the books he had read at that time on philosophy; then he goes on: "I can swear that since I came out of school I have never read any more of it."[23] From which we may conclude that in philosophy he remained a schoolboy.

In truth, though he likes to speak of his philosophical studies—was, indeed, proud of them—yet he was never really a philosopher. He had no serious interest in philosophical doctrines in themselves, but only in their bearing upon the dogmas of the Faith and these dogmas he accepted with unquestioning trust and submissiveness, without seeking to penetrate their depths. In any case, while he was doing his philosophy in Rome he still knew too little Greek to read the philosophers themselves in the original. He tells us that he knew them only by the translations, quotations, or summaries made by Latin writers, particularly Cicero, Brutus and Seneca.[24] In short, if he read the philosophers

---

22. *Epist.* 50, 1.
23. *Apologia contra Rufinum*, I, 30.
24. *Apologia contra Rufinum*, III, 39.

SAINT JEROME: THE EARLY YEARS

it was as a scholar, curious to learn what had been said on this or that question. Like the generality of the Romans, he was content to take note of diverse opinions, not bothering to confirm them or refute them or harmonise them.

Yet there was one part of philosophy—dialectics—which took firm hold of him in youth and counted for much in the formation of his mind. He loved to show that he knew its principles, its methods, its subtle distinctions. For dialectics—blood relation of rhetoric—furnished that warlike mind of his with a weapon. He used it vigorously in his polemics. For Jerome, as for many other Romans, the whole body of philosophy was fundamentally no more than an annexe of rhetoric.

Very different was Augustine's attitude. After his conversion as before it, the great African always went to the heart of doctrines. While still a student he mastered, without a teacher, the *Categories* of Aristotle. The reading of Cicero's *Hortensius* sufficed to set the direction of his moral life. It was by their teaching on the origin of evil that the Manicheans won him, by philosophy and science that he gradually broke away from them. For one moment he lingered in scepticism, only to refute it in his *Dialogues.* At last neo-Platonism brought him close to Christianity, and into Christianity he brought much neo-Platonic teaching. This long intellectual evolution covers almost the whole of Augustine's youth. We can find nothing comparable in the mind of the youthful Jerome. Augustine was a profound thinker; Jerome was, before all things, a scholar.

Apart from dialectic then, the influence of philosophical studies upon Jerome was superficial. That of the grammarians and rhetoricians went much deeper. Under Donatus he had been initiated into Latin classical literature—which he knew as no other man of his day knew it—and into all the mysteries of style. With the rhetoricians he developed his powers of oratory and polemic. But to these masters he owed likewise his faults as a writer: the over-use of erudition, the abuse of rhetoric.

Rhetoric, indeed, he had absorbed to such a point that he was never able to cast it off altogether. He bore its yoke not only in the detail of style, but in the processes of composition, in the way his theme developed, sometimes even—as in his panegyrics of holy men—in the conception of his subject. He knew it himself and sought to anticipate or disarm criticism by amusing *mea culpa*'s. From the desert where he was living the hard life of an anchorite he had written his friend Heliodorus a letter, eloquent but in places over-emphatic, urging that he should join him.[25] Later he said of this letter: "In that youthful work I was writing for my own pleasure. I was still all hot from study and the teaching of the rhetoricians; over some things I

---

25. *Epist.* 14.

SAINT JEROME: THE EARLY YEARS

strewed the flowers of the school."[26] The rhetorician's pupil lived on in the hermit: lived on, to the end, in the Abbot of Bethlehem.

Thus from his student days the intellectual physiognomy of Jerome begins to take shape. He was not to be an original thinker, nor a philosopher, nor a theologian; but a scholar, a controversialist, a man of letters. Grace did the rest.

---

26. *Epist.* 52, 1.

PART II

§

FROM SCHOOL TO THE DESERT

INTRODUCTORY

AT nineteen Jerome had finished his studies with the rhetoricians and philosophers and was still no more than a hard-working cheerful student with life before him; his thoughts and his ambitions were of the normal worldly sort and he was ready to follow obediently as his family might ordain—to direct his life either towards the higher civil service or towards the attractive combination of glory and high fees that goes with the profession of advocate.

Nine years later, become an ascetic, he had chosen to leave his own country to live the life of a hermit in a Syrian desert. We must follow the stages of this surprising evolution—as much moral as religious—whereby the Roman student had come to renounce the notable career which the future seemed to hold in store for him, and go off to bury himself at the age of twenty-eight in that far-off solitude.

CHAPTER I

BAPTISM

JEROME tells us[1] that he was baptised in Rome while he was a student of philosophy—probably in 366, on Easter Saturday. He was then round about the age of nineteen.

These late baptisms, surprising as they are to us now, were then almost the rule, even in good Christian families. The reason was not that which has been urged against early baptism in certain other churches—namely, the necessity of waiting till years of discretion, that baptism might be the candidate's own considered choice. It was a reason of the practical—almost cynical—order. Baptism, of course, effaced all sins committed before it. But one could not be sure of the complete remission of sins committed after it. Given the doubt, it was better to wait. So reasoned even as holy a woman as Augustine's mother. While a man felt young, he remained a catechumen, enjoying with untroubled mind the pleasures of this world. But with faith gone, health less certain, and old age upon

---

1. *Epist.* 15, 1; 16, 2.

him, a man began to think of putting himself right with heaven.

Jerome's parents were not very pious, and this is probably the reason why their oldest son, though a Christian in principle, was still unbaptised at nineteen.

But before going with him to the edge of the baptismal font, let us glance at his moral life up to that point.

It had not been very edifying. During his childhood at Stridon Jerome seems to have given little enough thought to Christianity. More or less consciously, he shared in the religious indifference of his parents, who were Catholics, but whose moral outlook was of a rough and ready practicality, the interests of heaven being decidedly second to the interests of this world. At Rome, in his early years as a student, he had shown himself as avid for pleasure as for study. He adored shows of every sort. No species of distraction came amiss to him, not even the pranks of the younger boys.

His approach to manhood was tempestuous, with amorous adventure and carnal pleasures. The memory of these things followed him even to the desert, disturbing the course of his austerities, sharpening with remorse the edge of his mortifications. In his own despite, temptations came, in which his imagination pictured the "delights of Rome" and himself mingling with bands of girls.[2] It would be a

---

2. *Epist.* 22, 7.

SAINT JEROME: THE EARLY YEARS

bad mistake to figure the student as a little model of the saint he was to be.

Yet it may well be that in the ardour of his repentance Jerome exaggerated his youthful sins. In a series of letters written mainly during his first period in the East he reproaches himself bitterly for the disorders of those earlier days. He declares that he is "soiled with all the filth of sins, lying in the sepulchre of crimes."[3] For his salvation, he says, his only hope lies in the infinite mercy of our Lord, who perhaps will one day say to him, as to Lazarus: "Jerome, come forth."[4] He adds that he had fallen "on the slippery road of youth"[5]; that he had come out to the desert to expiate his evil deeds[6]; that he shut himself up in this awful solitude "for fear of hell."[7] Eighteen years after the end of his student days, when he was a second time on the point of setting out for the East, he wrote: "Some consider me a criminal, loaded with all infamy; and this is naught in comparison with my sins."[8] As Abbot of Bethlehem he said bluntly in the course of a controversy: "If I praise virginity to the skies, it is not that I have it; but I admire what I have not."[9] At fifty,

---

3. *Epist.* 4, 2.
4. *Epist.* 7, 3; 4, 2.
5. *Epist.* 7, 4.
6. *Epist.* 15, 2.
7. *Epist.* 22, 7.
8. *Epist.* 45, 1.
9. *Epist.* 48, 20.

looking back upon his youth, he repeated the refrain of his *mea culpa*: "We have abandoned great cities to weep in the solitude of the fields the sins of our youth."[10]

Certainly Jerome knew better than we the events of his past. Yet it would surely be a mistake to interpret these confessions of his too literally. In the first place, allowance must be made for his own natural tendency to over-emphasis. Then, among the Christians of that time, it was a fashion to deepen the blackness of past errors, this being indeed a way of exalting the Divine mercy: the deeper the gulf, the greater the gratitude due to God who had drawn the sinner out of it. It was in some sense a convention—there are many instances of it in St. Augustine's *Confessions*.

What seems to confirm this reading in St. Jerome's case is that often, precisely when he is being hardest upon himself, he is simply reproducing Biblical expressions or paraphrasing another writer. In certain instances he is merely making a collective *mea culpa* as a member of the human race, without any special emphasis on his own sins. Thus there is a passage[11] often urged as proof that his life of dissipation had continued even after his baptism, whereas in fact he is not speaking of himself at all since he does no more than paraphrase a commentary of Origen upon Isaiah.

---

10. *Contra Johannem Hierosolymitanum*, 41.
11. *Epist.* 18, 11.

SAINT JEROME: THE EARLY YEARS

Thus, while we must take note of his manifold admissions as to the sins of his youth, we must not be misled by his exaggerations or his rhetorical figures. He had become an ascetic, but he remained a rhetorician; and he judged and condemned the follies of his past with a severity all the greater because the memories of them, dragging behind him like a chain, retarded his march towards the Christian ideal. The truth probably is that in his student days he was like many of his fellows: he was neither a criminal nor an angel; he was young, he thought more of the present than of the future, earth was nearer to him than heaven. In any case, he had both his ambition and his love of study to preserve him from the worst excesses, and he had the friendship of that very cream of the student body—all scholars, all to be ascetics—who were, as we have seen, his closest companions. Above all, during the last three years of his time in Rome he found the best of moral safeguards in his awakening religious sense.

He does not say how this awakening came about. Probably there was some disappointment—in love perhaps; emotional in any case—followed by a nervous reaction; then an instinctive turning back to the simple faith of his childhood, with a new interest in the rich basilicas of Rome and their moving ceremonies. Indeed, from this time the ardent devotion of the papal city seems to have produced a profound impression on him. He recalled it later: "One praises the faith of the Roman people. Where beside can one see such eagerness, such a pouring of people into the churches and round the tombs of the martyrs? Where can the *Amen* be heard to resound as it resounds in Rome, with a noise of thunder shaking the empty temples of the idols? With the Romans, devotion is greater and faith more unquestioning."[12]

Gradually Jerome's soul began to vibrate in harmony with the echoes of this popular piety. He began seriously to study Holy Writ. Thirty years later he tells us that from his youth up he had never let a day pass without "meditating on the Law, the Prophets, the Gospels and the [acts and writings of the] Apostles."[13]

But to begin with, left to himself and dazzled by the philosophy he had been taught, he formed a peculiar idea of Christianity—thinking he found in it, so he tells us later, the doctrines of Pythagoras, Plato and Empedocles.[14] The Abbot of Bethlehem was not proud of the philosophical divagations of the Roman student.

In this adventurous conception of Christianity, as in the enthusiastic picture he draws of the popular devotion of the Romans, we see his imagination at work: the imagination which was to inspire such splendid pages and

---

12. *Comment. in Epist. ad Galatas*, II, Praefat.
13. *Epist.* 50, 1.
14. *Epist.* 84, 6; *Apologia contra Rufinum*, III, 39.

SAINT JEROME: THE EARLY YEARS

unchain so many thunders round his head. It certainly had its part in the evolution which brought him to the faith.

Notice, for example, his description of the catacombs, wherein he loved to walk on Sundays with other students. "At Rome,"[15] he says, "in my youth, while I was pursuing the study of the liberal arts, it was my custom, on Sunday, with companions of my own age whose aspirations were like mine, to visit the tombs of the Apostles and martyrs. Often we entered crypts hollowed deep in the earth, where the path runs between bodies buried in the walls on either side. All is so dark that one feels the word of the Prophet almost realised: 'Let them go down living into hell.' From point to point glides down from above a ray of light to relieve the horror of the blackness; not so much a window, one feels, as a hole pierced by the light itself as it falls. Then you return, stepping carefully in the dark night that wraps you round, recalling Virgil's line: *horror ubique animos, simul ipsa silentia terrent.*"[16]

Pause for a moment on this description of the catacombs, triply interesting as history, literature, psychology.

Apart from a few dry references in ecclesiastical documents, Jerome is the one ancient writer to speak of the catacombs. What he has to say, therefore, is precious for

---

15. *Comment. in Ezechiel*, XIII, 40, 5.
16. *Aeneid*, II, 755.

Christian archaeology. He shows in what state were the underground cemeteries of Rome before the restoring work of Pope Damasus. And he shows that the characteristic features have not changed.

Looking at the thing as literature, we observe that Jerome, fourteen hundred years before Chateaubriand, felt the poetry of the catacombs. To set living before our eyes the memory of his own underground walks—and ours—a few lines, a few words suffice. It is the authentic touch of a master writer. Look, for contrast, at the commonplace fresco in the Invalides in which Bon Boulogne thinks he has recreated the scene, *St. Jerome Visiting the Catacombs*; it is amazing that the artist should have drawn so little profit from the vision sketched in a few vivid lines by his hero.

In the third place, these walks in the catacombs reveal a state of his mind. Up till now there had been practically nothing to indicate in Jerome the interior working of Christianity. Brought up in a Catholic family—but Catholic only by tradition and in name—he had remained a catechumen of the first degree, not particularly interested in the faith, absorbed in his studies and the ambition of secular success. These Sunday walks in the catacombs open up a new line of vision into the depths of his soul. Probably without his awareness he was slowly evolving towards the faith. He had been a Christian externally, his one link with the Church a list of catechumens on which his name appeared; gradually

SAINT JEROME: THE EARLY YEARS

he was turning into a Christian in mind and will, which of necessity quickly brought him to become one in fact.

The day came soon when he felt that he was ready for baptism. Then, with no apparent hesitation, he had his name inscribed on the list of *competentes*, catechumens of the second degree, those who wished to be baptised and were being instructed to that end.

A few months later he was baptised in Rome, probably with his friend Bonosus, of whom he was later to say: "He was once a recruit with me"—a *tiro*—that is, in the language of the Christians of the time, a neophyte, one newly baptised.[17]

The date of Jerome's baptism can be fixed with fair certainty. He received the sacrament in the course of his philosophical studies; therefore it was in one or other of his last two years in Rome, in 366 or 367, at Easter time, as was the custom. The year 367 can be eliminated. In his correspondence with Pope Damasus, in two places he recalls his baptism at Rome,[18] yet does not say (as one would expect) that he received the sacrament at the hands of Damasus—whence we must conclude that he received it from another pope. Now Damasus, who reigned over the Church of Rome till the year 384, began his reign in the autumn of 366, after

---

17. *Epist.* 3, 5.
18. *Epist.* 15, 1; 16, 2.

the death of Liberius, who died on September 24 of that year. Jerome then must have been baptised by Pope Liberius in 366, on Easter Saturday.

Several painters have essayed to recreate Jerome's baptism: they have not succeeded very well. There is nothing to be said for Bon Boulogne's fresco at the Invalides, which is no better than its neighbour, the *Visit to the Catacombs*, and is indeed one of the most disappointing things in this Chapel of St. Jerome. The same subject is to be seen at Rome, on the Janiculan, on one of the frescoes of the outer portico of the church of Sant'Onofrio. It is by Domenichino and is of interest for the history of art, because one can see in it a kind of first sketch of a real masterpiece by the same painter—*The Last Communion of St. Jerome*. But the comparison is of itself enough to show up the artificiality in the picture of the baptism. The architectural framework, the attitudes of the personages, the declamatory gesture of the neophyte and the clerics—the whole thing is conventional, lacking all contact with real times and places.

Really to recall the scene, we must begin by giving it its proper setting in a baptistery of the time. It is of small use to look for one in Rome, where the Christian monuments have been so completely worked over that one can with difficulty detect an occasional trace of the original buildings. In Africa, on the other hand, the old baptisteries brought to light some thirty years since look very much as they looked

SAINT JEROME: THE EARLY YEARS

in the beginning. Take as an example the one at Djemila (to the west of Constantine), discovered in 1922 and dating, as it happens, from the time of Jerome. It is remarkably well preserved; either in position or close by were found all the elements of the construction and the decoration, and it was possible to reconstruct it right up to the roof. The walls, of brick, are covered on the inside with stucco, like the pillars. The ground is covered all over with mosaics, wherein are pious inscriptions. With the buildings attached—including a complete bathing establishment for the catechumens (warm rooms, a cold room with piscinaes, heating arrangements, and the rest), the shape is an irregular quadrilateral, nearly rectangular. The baptistery proper is a large rotunda, with two colonnades jutting out from it on opposite sides. It is in three concentric divisions. First, an encircling corridor with two vestibules, a corridor whose two walls have set in them thirty-six semi-circular niches, decorated with large stone crosses and shells fixed in the stucco; it was probably a dressing-place for the catechumens. Second is the central rotunda, covered by a cupola, and having a balcony at the top; there is an opening for light in the cupola, and a ring from which the lamp was hung. Lastly, in the centre of the rotunda is the baptismal font, square, surrounded by a dais likewise square, resting on four columns. This font had two steps leading down into it. It was covered all over with mosaic. On the bottom were fish, symbolic of baptism, and of the faithful. All round, a broad rim bearing on three sides—north, east and south—an inscription relating to the ceremony. The catechumen would come straight from the bath, his naked body covered by white veils, and go down into the font by the steps on the west side, facing the east where was the bishop who, surrounded by his clergy, proceeded to the ceremony. Once the rites of baptism were over, the neophyte passed on to an adjoining room—the *consignatorium*—where he received confirmation. His white garments, symbol of purity, he retained till the end of the week following—the *sabbatum in albis*.

That is the historical and architectural background against which one must imagine Jerome receiving baptism. Truth gains by these details, nor do the poetic and the picturesque suffer loss.

Those white garments were still in his mind ten years later in the desert. He wrote to Pope Damasus: "I held myself bound to consult the Chair of Peter and the faith praised by the mouth of the Apostle. Now I ask food for my soul from the spot where once I received the vestments of Christ."[19] He was proud of having been baptised in Rome by the Pope. He ever considered himself a Christian of Rome, forming his faith on that of the Roman Church.[20]

---

19. *Epist.* 15, 1.
20. *Christi vestem in Romana urbe suscipiens* (*Epist.* 16, 2). *A me homine Romano* (*Epist.* 15, 3).

SAINT JEROME: THE EARLY YEARS

Yet the importance of this sacrament for Jerome's future—even his specifically religious future—should not be exaggerated. In the account of his baptism no trace appears of hesitation or spiritual inquietude, no trace of an intellectual or even a real moral crisis or turning-point; nothing comparable to the conversion of Augustine. Born in a Christian family, Jerome had himself baptised as soon as he really felt that he was a Christian, for so his own conscience and the law of the Church required. That is all. From the baptismal font he did not emerge a new man. In the years immediately following, the influence of the sacrament on his thought seems not to have been particularly marked. He remained a not precisely worldly Christian, sincere in his religious feeling, but not aflame with it. The thing that really decided his future was his ascetic vocation; and this came several years later.

It is a curious circumstance that Jerome heard the call of grace, not at Rome as he came forth from the waters of baptism, but in Gaul, where he was travelling with one eye on secular study and one on secular advancement.

CHAPTER II

GAUL AND THE VOCATION TO ASCETICISM

EIGHTEEN months after his baptism, his Roman studies, as he tells us, being at an end, Jerome set out for Gaul with his friend Bonosus. The two friends made a notable stay at Treves. They pressed on "to the half-barbarous banks of the Rhine." They were absolutely inseparable—"one room, one table."[1]

They would have finished their studies in July 367. They were then twenty—the fateful age when, in accord with custom and scholastic regulations, the police had to see to it that they left Rome. Leave Rome they did, presumably with regret. First, one must suppose, they made for Stridon, to see their families and enjoy some period of vacation. But soon they were on the way to Gaul. With what object?

Almost certainly to lay the foundations of their future, to set their foot on a career, to please their families by finding a post in the administration. Neither of them had yet renounced the world. They knew that the Imperial offices

---

1. *Epist.* 3, 5.

SAINT JEROME: THE EARLY YEARS

drew their staff principally from young men leaving school. There was purpose in their going to Treves, for it was at that time, for the great part of the year, the capital of the Western Empire. As the menace of invasion from Germany grew more unmistakable, the centre of gravity of Gaul as of the Empire began to shift in the direction of the Rhine; from Lyons to Paris under Julian, from Paris to Treves under Valentinian. We hear from time to time of long periods spent by him in this town. Treves was a Roman colony in a Gallic area, and as early as the third century it had been the residence of the Gallo-Roman emperors. As a capital, it looked the part. To this day one can visit the imposing ruins of its imperial palace, the ramparts, gates, baths, amphitheatre. With the court, which frequently held its great assizes there, the central administrative offices had likewise settled. Jerome's family—like the family of Bonosus—probably had visions of the young man securing a post, with the influence of some patron in high place. Beyond that, the two friends must have had a second purpose of their own: they were keen scholars, and would assuredly have wished to advance their studies in the schools of Gaul; for these were then so famous that students flocked to them from Italy, in particular to the schools of Autun, Bordeaux and Treves.

We have no knowledge of the exact course of their journeyings. Jerome tells us only of his stay in Treves and on the banks of the Rhine, with an excursion north. But there are other places that he must have visited. To get to Treves he would have to cross the East of Gaul, at least part of the Lyonnaise and Belgium. He must have seen Autun—and even stayed there to hear the masters of its schools. Further, the many points of contact he had later in Aquitaine—of which we learn by his letters and dedications—make it seem probable that he knew the south-west, from Narbonne to Toulouse and Bordeaux.

During these wanderings over Gaul he was observant of customs, and notes down anything unusual. He even says that he saw a tribe of cannibals, the Alticotti, an aboriginal tribe of Brittany. The fact is very surprising, especially in the Gaul of that period. But the traveller is quite definite and goes into some detail; these cannibals were true gourmets: meeting a herd of pigs or a flock of sheep in the forest, they disdained the flesh of the animals and made their meal off the swineherd or the shepherdess—selecting the shepherdess' throat and the lower part of the swineherd's loins—and declaring both delicious.[2] Since Jerome says so, we may agree that he saw these savages, without feeling any certainty that he was ever at one of their banquets.

His interest was not confined to cannibals. As a good student, he had the curiosity to take lessons in the language of the country. He lent an ear to the speech of the people,

---

2. *Adversus Jovinianum*, II, 7.

SAINT JEROME: THE EARLY YEARS

to the Celtic dialects, still living, and he learnt at least the elements. Some years later, journeying over Asia Minor, he found that the language of the Galatians, so many hundred years after their emigration to the East, was still practically identical with that of the Treviri.[3]

In the towns of Gaul that he visited on his journey his ardour for study came upon him once more. He must have entered many schools, listened to many masters. Especially he never missed an opportunity to add to the library which he had begun to build up in Rome and which was very close to his heart. He would halt on his way to copy manuscripts, and this for his friends as well as himself. Thus at Treves, he tells us, he transcribed with his own hand for Rufinus two works of Hilary of Poitiers, the *Commentary on the Psalms* and the great collection of the *Synods*.[4]

When he muses over memories of Gaul it is always to Treves that he brings us back. There more than anywhere he stayed: in the neighbourhood of the court, as his family, with an eye to his preferment, had instructed him. But if he tried for a position, he did it half-heartedly; which explains why he did not get one. By way of compensation he found at Treves what he was not looking for—the key to his future destiny. There first he was overcome by grace.

---

3. *Comment. in Epist. ad Galatas*, II, Praefat.
4. *Epist.* 5, 2.

PAUL MONCEAUX

Treves was at that time not only the capital of Gaul and the intermittent capital of the empire, it was also a very centre of Christianity, even of asceticism after the oriental fashion. As early as 314 the town had a bishop, who took part in the Council of Arles. In 336 Athanasius of Alexandria was sent in banishment to Treves, and he made known the devotional practices of Egypt, the supernatural virtues of St. Anthony and St. Pachomius, of the anchorites and cenobites. In those days at the very gates of Treves hermits' huts might be seen. And incredible things happened in those huts. Into one of them, for instance, came two officers of the palace, who had chanced to walk that way; they never came out, for they renounced all things, even the love of their betrothed, who likewise consecrated themselves to God.[5]

We do not know if Jerome experienced some crisis of the sort at Treves. What is certain is that the influence of this centre of asceticism was too strong for him. It was there that he vowed himself to Christ, and to the same vow his example brought his friend Bonosus.[6] In this unexpected resolution he saw simply an effect of grace; but in that corner of Gaul where Athanasius had lived and where men still read his biography of the first anchorite, Jerome's

---

5. Augustine, *Confess.* VIII, 6, 15.
6. *Epist.* 3, 5.

SAINT JEROME: THE EARLY YEARS

imagination must assuredly have created visions of Oriental asceticism, with the radiant figure of St. Anthony in ecstasy. The very depths of his mind were possessed by the firm purpose of going one day to live as an anchorite in the East.

But he was at Treves and the East was far off. For the moment he had to be satisfied with a withdrawal from the world in his birthplace, in the company of chosen friends who shared alike his literary tastes and his aspirations towards the ascetic ideal.

CHAPTER III

AQUILEIA: THE CHOIR OF THE BLESSED

Upon his return to Stridon Jerome probably received a cool welcome from his family. Not only was he back empty-handed, having obtained nothing—and maybe solicited nothing—at the court; but here he was, turning his back on the brilliant worldly future of the family dreams, betraying the family interests for an ideal that any sane man could see to be chimerical! His parents and he no longer spoke the same language. Between them and him the initial difference of outlook caused an ever-widening gulf. It is not surprising that Jerome, obstinate by nature and not patient, made but a brief stay at Stridon.

In the neighbouring town of Aquileia, whither he was drawn by friendships of long standing, he knew he would find kindred souls. There he settled down. For three or four years he lived there happily, in a circle of rare spirits—ascetic and cultured—in the enchantment of a dream come true.

Aquileia, the chief port at the top of the Adriatic, the administrative and commercial centre of the whole district, was likewise the religious and literary centre. In the second

SAINT JEROME: THE EARLY YEARS

half of the fourth century several councils met there, with a particular eye to the defence of the Catholic Church against the official Arianism of Upper Italy and the Danubian provinces. For a moment heresy had conquered even the town of Aquileia: one of its bishops, the African Fortunatianus, had joined the semi-Arian party and by way of propaganda had composed brief commentaries on the Gospels in the Latin of the people. But after the death of Fortunatianus the wind had changed. His successor, Valerianus, the bishop known by Jerome, was a militant Catholic, who sought to stamp out Arianism in his diocese. In this undertaking he was effectively seconded by the priest Chromatius, who was to succeed him as bishop.

Chromatius was a friend and correspondent of Jerome, and to him Jerome dedicated several works. He was a man of much distinction: literary, a talented speaker (sermons of his have come down to us), a scholar particularly interested in works on scripture. More than all, he was the apostle of asceticism in those parts and practised what he preached.

Like Treves, from which Jerome had come, Aquileia was a centre of asceticism. Here again we are in the footsteps of that perpetual exile, Athanasius of Alexandria. He had lived there round the year 345, and had told marvellous stories of Egypt, of the anchorites, of St. Anthony. From that time Aquileia had its ascetics, particularly numerous, it seems, at the time of Jerome's sojourn.

PAUL MONCEAUX

The house of Chromatius was their meeting place. It was a sort of family monastery, where everybody practised asceticism—Chromatius and his brother Eusebius, their mother and their many sisters, all consecrated to God. Notable among those who frequented the house were three clerics of the town and a monk, with all of whom Jerome was later to correspond; the archdeacon Jovinus, the deacon Julianus, the sub-deacon Niceas (later a pilgrim to Jerusalem), and the monk Chrysocomas.

With this group of ascetics Jerome either made or renewed acquaintance in the home of Chromatius. His pleasure was the greater in that he found there three compatriots, the companions of his choice in Rome and still his closest friends. First, of course, Bonosus; he also, back from Gaul, had abandoned Stridon for Aquileia. Then Rufinus; he belonged to Concordia, a small town nearby, but he was seldom there, being one of Chromatius' most regular guests till he left for the East. The third was Heliodorus, who often came from Altinum, another town in the vicinity; after his studies in Rome he had entered the administration, then become a monk, but without leaving his family and with no thought of the desert.

To these more or less regular guests and to the inhabitants of Chromatius' house must be added friends who merely passed that way, but who likewise grew intimate with Jerome—such men as Paul of Concordia, Evagrios of

SAINT JEROME: THE EARLY YEARS

Antioch and Evagrios' shadow, the good and pious Innocentius, who was to die under Jerome's eyes in Syria.

Among other original qualities, Paul of Concordia was a centenarian—and a rather remarkable one, vigorous in health and keen of mind, and bursting with anecdote. He had a rich library, containing most of the Christian authors. He was that rare thing in bibliophiles, a ready lender of books; and he sometimes had much trouble in getting them back, even from ascetics. He had a special admiration for Tertullian, and he loved to tell a story which bore witness to the lasting influence of the great apologist. In his youth he said, he had known a cleric who had been St. Cyprian's secretary. From this man he had learnt that it was St. Cyprian's custom each day to read some pages of Tertullian, and that his way of asking for the book was to say: "*Da magistrum*—Hand me the master."[1]

Jerome, who has preserved the story for us, loved Paul, venerating him as a centenarian, flattering him a little as a book-collector. He likewise borrowed books from him, and even returned them. From his Syrian desert he made borrowings; and by way of thanks sent him the story of one whose name he shared—a copy of the *Life* of St. Paul the Hermit.[2]

---

1. Jerome, *De viris illustribus*, 53.
2. *Epist.* 10, 3.

PAUL MONCEAUX

Evagrios, priest and later Bishop of Antioch, was definitely a personage. He belonged to a noble family of Syria, made illustrious in the past by the General Pompeianus Francus, vanquisher of Queen Zenobia at Palmyra. Under Julian's rule, Evagrios had left his home in Antioch to journey to the West with the Bishop Eusebius of Vercelli, who was returning from exile. For ten years he had lived in Italy. He stood high in the esteem of Pope Damasus and the Emperor Valentinian. He even approached the emperor on the Pope's behalf, when the Pope was suffering unjust accusations. At Milan he checkmated the intrigues of the Arian bishop Auxentius. And he obtained from Valentinian pardon for an unfortunate woman of Vercelli who had been the victim of a miscarriage of justice. He was an able diplomat, and a writer and speaker of talent. We may still read his Latin translation of Athanasius's *Life of St. Anthony*. While he was at Aquileia, he edified people of ascetic life by his vivid accounts of the virtues of the cenobites and the feats of mortification of the hermits; and thereby he helped to give an eastward bent to the interest or vocation of Jerome and his friends, whose host he was to be at Antioch.

To complete the tale of people with whom Jerome was at this period in contact, mention must be made of the ascetics of Hemona, a small town to the north-east of Stridon. In that place he knew a monk called Antonius

SAINT JEROME: THE EARLY YEARS

and a group of nuns, holy women living in community. He wrote to them from the desert.[3]

All these friendships—new or renewed—were some consolation for the frigid reception he had met at Stridon. Practically in open quarrel with his family, more or less at war with the bishop and clergy of the place—on whom he spent much sarcasm—he had no love for the town of his birth. Yet he must have returned there from time to time, particularly to see his sister, for whom he showed warm affection. Certainly he aggravated the trouble in which he stood with his parents by the influence he exercised on this girl. He deliberately set about drawing her away from the world, which at first had attracted her, to win her for the ascetical life. And in the end he succeeded. He got her to put herself under the spiritual direction of Julianus, the deacon of Aquileia.[4] His sister, whom he saw at long intervals, was his one point of interest in Stridon.

Aquileia had completely conquered him. In the circle of ascetics he felt that he was in heaven. It was not precisely a community. It was a free companionship, with its centre at the house of Chromatius, where clergy and laity, people of piety and culture, met together—united in a common ideal by the same tastes, joining to the ardour of mysticism

---

3. *Epist.* 11 and 12.
4. *Epist.* 6, 2; 7, 4.

the delights of the intellect. It was already something like the circle of Marcella on the Aventine, or rather like Augustine's home at Tagaste after his conversion. Jerome later (373) noted in his *Chronicle*: "The clergy of Aquileia are like a choir of the blessed."[5]

---

5. *Chron. ad ann.* 373.

CHAPTER IV

DEPARTURE FOR THE EAST

SUDDENLY, about the beginning of 374, the "choir of the blessed" broke up. The ascetics dispersed. Jerome set out for the East, with the intention of going on pilgrimage to Jerusalem and then living in the desert as a hermit.

It is generally agreed that this sudden departure was caused by a breach between Jerome and his parents and some of his associates. This breach had already begun some time before with his conversion to the ascetic life; it had been made definite by his determination to win his sister to the same way of life and by the quarrels that flowed from his effort. His parents clearly could not forgive him for having ruined the future they had dreamed for him, by renouncing worldly ambition and burying himself in a devotion which could only seem to them sterile. They were even more furious with him for having added to the disorganisation of family schemes, by drawing his sister off on the same silly path. Further, we can well believe that Jerome's haughty and intractable character—and his mordant wit—helped to add bitterness to a difference of outlook already sufficiently fundamental. At any rate it is at this time that he begins to discover that there are "enemies" about him, and to say so. Already mistrustful, he took to suspecting intrigues or plots, not only at Stridon, but at Aquileia, and even at Hemona, among the priests, the monks and the consecrated virgins.[1]

Nevertheless, neither the suspiciousness of his temper, nor the family differences and quarrels, nor the alleged intrigues of real or imagined enemies, are enough to account for what happened. There must have been something else.

Notice first that Jerome was not the only one to leave suddenly; the whole group at Aquileia was broken up. Seven of them at least left the country, each choosing his own place, for varying lengths of time, going as far off as Egypt, Palestine, Syria. Rufinus sailed off to Egypt, where he joined Antonia Melania, the famous Melania the Elder, a great lady of much piety and a tendency to command; he became her spiritual director, her secretary, and to some extent her factotum. Bonosus became a hermit on a rocky islet in the Adriatic. Heliodorus made the pilgrimage to Jerusalem; and so did Niceas, separately. Evagrios went home to Antioch, along with Innocentius. Thus at least six friends of Jerome left Aquileia as he did, and there is no ground for supposing that it was in pursuance of an agreement come to among them.

---

1. *Epist.* 6 and 11–12.

SAINT JEROME: THE EARLY YEARS

What had happened? Jerome himself, in a letter to Rufinus written a year later, speaks of a whirlwind which bore them off (*subitus turbo convolvit*), and of an impious rending which tore them apart (*impia distraxit convulsio*).[2] It seems then that there was some violent cause for this separation of friends. How did it come about?

At that time, in practically all the churches of the West, the majority of the clergy were still hostile to the new asceticism imported from the East. Further, the Arian party, favoured by the Empress Justina, was then very powerful in the north of Italy, and the civil authorities were very ready to do as it wished. Now Jerome and his friends were rigidly orthodox, declared enemies of the Arians, against whom Chromatius with Evagrios waged a vigorous campaign.[3] Regarded with unfriendly eyes by the Catholic clergy as a whole, the ascetics of Aquileia were at the mercy of the Arians, who, supported as at Milan by the empress, were in a position to pick a quarrel and set the civil authorities in action against them. This would explain the "whirlwind," the "impious rending"—the display of force, that is, and the order to disperse.

It remains to explain, however, what were the attacks and the calumnies of his fellow-countrymen—of which

---

2. *Epist.* 3, 3.
3. *Epist.* 1, 15; 7, 6.

Jerome complained so bitterly and before which he fled to the East. Unpleasant rumours were in circulation about him. Mysterious accusations, whispered in corners, were listened to seriously by serious people, even in those ascetical groups where Jerome should have been defended. He tells us himself that the monk Antonius and the consecrated virgins of Hemona had broken off all relations with him and no longer replied to his letters.[4] Of what could he have been accused?

Young, ardent and impetuous was Jerome. And he had probably been guilty of some imprudence in conduct and thereby exposed himself to calumny. He always exercised a strange influence over women and always found pleasure in their society. Grown older, he was the oracle of the Roman great ladies of the Aventine circle; and even then, in spite of the halo of the one-time hermit, in spite of his position as spiritual director, in spite of his duties as secretary to the Pope, there was scandalous talk about his relations with Paula, herself a woman of much holiness and the mother of five children. Later still, when he was abbot at Bethlehem, he was accused of writing too much for women, of dedicating most of his works to them. In fact we shall always find at his side some angel guardian—this same Paula, for instance, her daughter Eustochium, then her granddaughter,

---

4. *Epist.* 11 and 12.

SAINT JEROME: THE EARLY YEARS

likewise Paula. At the age of twenty-five he was neither less attractive nor, when he chose, less agreeable. Probably he enjoyed, rather more than was discreet, the company of certain pious women, not in the very heart of the "choir of the blessed!" Hence the unpleasant comments, at which he expresses such irritation in his letters. Hence also the cold silence of the virgins of Hemona, and the scandalised indignation of his Aunt Castorina.[5] In vain Jerome protested his innocence, calling the Saviour to witness. In spite of all the bites of vipers, he cried: "I fear not the judgment of men; I shall have God for judge."[6] Which did not stop men judging or vipers biting.

What made things worse was Jerome's uncompromising and mistrustful character, his intractability and his caustic wit. He never admitted, for he never grasped, that anyone could sincerely and honestly differ in opinion from him. If later on, as far as Bethlehem from Hippo, he all but quarrelled with Augustine, whom he had never seen, we may guess what a reception he was likely to give in his youth to the objections or criticisms of people in Stridon, Hemona or Aquileia. Remember how he spoke of Lupicinus, the Bishop of Stridon, whom he compared in rapid succession to a sick pilot, a blind man, an ass, a pot-lid.[7] It would have

---

5. *Epist.* 13.
6. *Epist.* 6, 2.
7. *Epist.* 7, 5.

needed the patience of an angel not to cherish any resentment, and Lupicinus was probably not of the angelic sort. The fact is, Jerome was too witty for an ascetic. In his own despite, the cutting word slipped out. Unable to stand up to him, his victims got what vengeance they could by slander and calumny. He would have had fewer enemies if he had been more patient, more master of his tongue and his pen.

With the light shed on the matter by his character and the history of the time, Jerome's sudden resolution to go off to the desert is no longer a mystery. Unable to remain in Aquileia, unwilling to settle in Stridon, where he was so unfavourably regarded, he decided to go to the East, that sacred land of asceticism which had filled his dreams since his vocation at Treves.

Before starting he had, of course, to go to Stridon and say good-bye to his family. This last visit must have been stormy; for when he went off, the breach between himself and his people was final. From now on they broke off all communication. Two years later we find him writing from the desert to Julianus of Aquileia: "Here where I am now I am not only ignorant of what is happening in my native place, but even if my native place still exists."[8]

He left the town in the spring of 374. He never saw it again. Four years later Italy was all but submerged by the

---

8. *Epist.* 6.

SAINT JEROME: THE EARLY YEARS

invading Goths. The wave broke this time against the rampart of the Julian Alps and the Roman legions; but the barbarians, following their custom, avenged their failure by laying waste the country. Stridon they destroyed completely. Of this devastation Jerome says: "Witness the soil of my birthplace; apart from the sky and the earth, the bushes springing again and the thickets, all has perished."[9] He was exaggerating a little, since later he sent his brother "to his birthplace to sell some small half-ruined farms which had escaped the hands of the barbarians."[10] For all that, the unhappy city had so thoroughly received its death-blow, that today we know not even where it stood.

At the time of his setting out for the East Jerome was about twenty-seven. Intellectually he was still only a rhetorician with a desire for learning. Morally he had just undergone a profound transformation. From the time of his baptism, and still more from the time of his vocation at Treves and in his retreat at Aquileia, he had realised the seriousness of life and the greatness of Christianity. He had resolved to follow the way that would assure his salvation. At the same time the dominant traits of his character take clearer shape—ardour for study, generosity of soul, enthusiasm, devotion to his friends; all these and certain less

---

9. *Comment. in Sophoniam*, I, 2.
10. *Epist.* 66, 14.

good—intractability, prejudice, mistrust and resentment. He set off as a pilgrim—but discontented, embittered, at quarrel with his family and many of his compatriots. He flies before calumnies or the shadow of enmities; but always about him, behind him, he hears hatred prowling and the hissing of "vipers."

His first goal was Antioch; after that Jerusalem; then the desert of Syria. There is a tradition that gives him two or three companions on the journey, but there is no justification for it; he seems definitely to have set off alone. Much as he rejoiced in friendship, he never feared solitude, being of those upon whom solitude never bears heavily because it is peopled with their thoughts, their memories, and their dreams.

For his long journey he had the choice between two routes: the sea route—by the Adriatic and the Eastern Mediterranean; the land route—which has been practically closed these fifteen centuries to Europeans, but is now being opened up by the railways. Like a good pilgrim, Jerome chose the land. He set down his itinerary, with some faint repugnance at the memory of the length and the fatigues of the journey. "At last," he says, "after having led a wandering life in the uncertainty of my journeyings, after having travelled through Thrace, Pontus and Bithynia, the whole of Galatia, Cappadocia and Cilicia, my body broken by the burning heat, at last I reached Syria,

SAINT JEROME: THE EARLY YEARS

which to me was like a peaceful harbour open to the shipwrecked sailor."[11]

Arm-chair travellers have felt called upon to make the criticism that Jerome wandered haphazard, at the whim of circumstance. In reality, it would seem that he went to Antioch by the shortest road, the ordinary road: from Aquileia to Dyrrachium, by the Adriatic or Dalmatia; from Dyrrachium to Constantinople, by the military road which cut straight across the Balkan peninsula; from the Bosphorus to Syria, by the great road over the plateaux of Asia Minor. His route then was not abnormal. It was the postal road.

The journey, all the worse because it was summer, seemed to Jerome very fatiguing, interminable; the more so because, while an important personage, a high official, say, or a tax farmer, could use the imperial post, the ordinary man travelled on foot. Besides, the young ascetic had chosen to travel as a pilgrim, a soldier of Christ, as he says.[12] But when he reached the gates of Antioch he was at the end of his strength, worn down, broken, ill. He had to stop—Jerusalem drifted very far off in a mirage.

---

11. *Epist.* 3, 3.
12. *Epist.* 22, 30.

CHAPTER V

THE CHARMS OF ANTIOCH

ANTIOCH was at that time one of the three great cities of the East, rival to Constantinople and Alexandria. A favourite residence of the emperors, an administrative and military centre, a workshop of all the industries, the emporium of an immense trade, it was the real capital for Syria and the neighbouring regions; very populous, sumptuous and full of colour, gay, splendid with broad avenues, sacred groves, magnificent buildings, statues and frescoes under dazzling porticos, art collections, libraries and famous schools. Vigorously and even tumultuously alive, it was endlessly agitated by the movement of a population very mixed, turbulent and always ready for riot. For all that country it was the meeting-place of state officials, army officers, financiers and men of business, adventurers, harlots, and the merely idle, artists and men of letters. It was likewise the pantheon or the meeting-ground of the most diverse religions, the fortress of Graeco-Oriental paganism, the battle-ground of the heresies and sects of Christendom.

SAINT JEROME: THE EARLY YEARS

For Jerome, worn out from his long journey, this great town, noisy and storm-tossed as it was, yet seemed, as he says: "a peaceful harbour open to the shipwrecked sailor."[1] He arrived in the autumn of 374, and went straight to the house of his friend Evagrios, who had preceded him there and was waiting for him. In that vast and opulent house, rich in books, rich in the virtues, he was welcomed as a guest sent by God, with the cordiality due to a confrère, and all the refinements of Eastern hospitality. He stayed there a year, rebuilding his health, working, attending lectures, writing—slipping off sometimes on excursions in the neighbourhood, especially that domain of Maronia which belonged to Evagrios, where the monk Malchus was seen in person by his future panegyrist.[2]

Jerome's host rendered him another service—a service of some importance for a good Catholic newly come from the West. He saved him from *faux pas*—thereby saving him from many a sting in that wasps' nest, Christian Antioch. The town, which was to have four bishops at once, already had three of them, and all three claimed to be Catholic. First Meletius, elected by acclamation in 361 with the help of the Arianisers, and upheld by the majority of the Churches of the East. Then Euzoios, consecrated by Arians

---

1. *Epist.* 3, 3.
2. *Vita Malchi* 2.

PAUL MONCEAUX

thinly disguised. Third Paulinus, chosen by the Eustathians or uncompromising Catholics, ordained in 362 by Lucifer of Calaris and supported by the Church of Alexandria and by the Church of Rome. A Christian coming from Italy would assuredly have been considerably embarrassed to find the real bishop. But, immediately on his return to Antioch, Evagrios had joined the party of Paulinus, Pope Damasus' protégé. Evagrios' bishop, the pope's man. Those two things settled the question for Jerome. He established relations with Paulinus, who became his friend, and a few years later ordained him priest. Fundamentally he had little interest in these Eastern quarrels; since his baptism he regarded himself as a Christian of Rome.

What interested him more was either to find already in Antioch or to welcome as later-comers several of his friends from Aquileia. Innocentius was there before him, having probably come back with Evagrios. Next to appear was the sub-deacon Niceas, who had seen Jerusalem; Jerome made several excursions with him. Heliodorus had likewise gone straight to Jerusalem. Wearied out by the journey, he had fallen ill there. Nursed back to health by the devoted care of the Latin monk Florentinus, he came to Antioch, remained there some considerable time, but resisted Jerome's vigorous efforts to drag him off to the desert. The group of friends found endless pleasure in their common memories of Aquileia.

SAINT JEROME: THE EARLY YEARS

Unhappily death was prowling about them. Innocentius fell seriously ill: a malignant fever carried him off. Soon after it was the turn of another of their companions, Hylas, a virtuous man, servant of Antonia Melania, sent by her to Syria to bring aid to the Egyptians exiled there for their orthodoxy. This double loss was a cruel blow to Jerome, devoted to his friends and himself not fully recovered after his journey. He attached himself all the more closely to his host, who redoubled his attentions to him, so that Jerome could say: "I enjoyed our dear Evagrios, yet was afflicted that, being always ill, I was a new burden upon him."[3]

"Always ill," is the burden of his letters at that time. In Syria, he wrote to Rufinus: "I have been stricken by all possible maladies."[4] And to Julianus of Aquileia: "My continual sufferings, maladies of the body as well as griefs of the mind, so consumed me that death lay in wait for me and I almost lost consciousness of myself."[5] That he escaped the fate of Innocentius and Hylas was a miracle.

Yet he worked, and worked hard, to add to his learning in that great centre of scholarship. He began by learning Greek thoroughly, for till then he had known it but ill. Then he began the study of exegesis, following the lectures of Apollinaris, one of the most celebrated masters of the

---

3. *Epist.* 3, 3.
4. Ibid. 3.
5. *Epist.* 6.

time. This Apollinaris was Bishop of Laodicea, but he was more often in Antioch than in his diocese. He taught with great success, commenting on the Scriptures with a learning which was the marvel of his hearers. He was already suspect of heresy, but was not yet considered a heretic; it was not till two years later, in 376, that he separated himself from the Church and ordained his supporter Vitalis as Bishop of Antioch. Jerome therefore had no scruple about attending his lectures. Without bothering about the hazardous teachings of the theologian on the nature of Christ, he admired the learning of the exegete and the originality of his method. He noted his explanations of obscure passages of Scripture, his refutations of Porphyry and other opponents of Christianity. Later he made many borrowings from him for his commentaries on the books of scripture.

During this time at Antioch Jerome made his début—a very modest début—as a writer, in literature and exegesis. The oldest of his works, so far as we know, is a curious little story, edifying if macabre, known by the name of *The Miracle of Vercelli*. His theme was the story, then quite recent, of a judicial error followed by supernatural happenings which gave the heroine the appearance of a martyr. A woman of Vercelli, in North Italy, had been unjustly accused of adultery and cited, along with a young man said to be her partner in guilt, before the tribunal of the governor of the province. As was usual, they were both put to the torture to force

SAINT JEROME: THE EARLY YEARS

them to confess. The suffering proving too much for him, the young man admitted that he was guilty; but to the end the woman affirmed her innocence. Both were condemned to death. At the first stroke of the sword, the young man gave up the ghost. But the executioners for some time did their uttermost against the woman in vain; she seemed as though protected by an unseen hand; seven separate times they tried. In the end, however, the poor woman fell lifeless. As night had come, the officers went home, postponing the legal burial till the next day. In their absence, certain priests, filled with compassion, watched by the corpse. Suddenly they perceived that the dead woman was breathing. Then, in the tomb already prepared, they laid the body of an old woman who had just died, very conveniently. They carried off the resurrected woman and hid her in a country house. So well was she cared for that she completely regained her health. Still she remained under sentence of death, in danger of execution. She was finally freed from danger by the intervention of Evagrios, Jerome's friend, who happened to be at Vercelli and used his influence with the emperor to secure her pardon.

The story had made some stir, especially in Christian circles in Italy. Towards the end of 374, urged on by Innocentius, who reproached him with letting his talent lie dormant and suggested this subject, Jerome decided to set down for the public the story of the woman who had been seven times stricken by the executioners and miraculously saved. He seized the occasion, as he said, to get the rust off his style, and also to express his gratitude to his host Evagrios, who had played so notable a part in the affair.

The work is prefaced by a dedication to Innocentius, a dedication somewhat in the form of a letter; as a letter it comes first in his correspondence, and so has come down to us.[6] The thing is not a masterpiece. The style is brilliant, but the narration is artificial, constructed from end to end according to the rules of the school, embellished with all the flowers of rhetoric—too many descriptions, discourses and dialogues, too many invocations, exclamations, metaphors and antitheses. In a word, it is the work of a rhetorician, with all the faults of its kind; yet there are hints of talent to come, and even of talent realised.

The other work composed by Jerome at Antioch is now lost—which is precisely what the author would have wished, as we shall see. It was an essay in exegesis, a *Commentary on Obadiah*. The prophecy of Obadiah, the shortest of the old Testament books, contains the recital of a vision, wherein maledictions are heaped up against the Idumaeans, the enemies of Israel. The theme lent itself to amplification and declamation; so that the tyro in exegesis, still unemancipated from the school, flung himself upon

---

6. *Epist.* 1.

SAINT JEROME: THE EARLY YEARS

it greedily. He gave rein to his rhetoric, seeing allegories everywhere, thundering against the enemies of God who were identified only too easily with the enemies of Jerome. At the time, with the fever of inspiration hot on him, he was enchanted with these first steps in exegesis. Later he was considerably less proud of them. By then a master in that field, he was a severe critic and he regretted this early outburst. Heroically he sacrificed his masterpiece, burned his manuscript, and hoped to hear no more of it.

Twenty years later, as abbot in Bethlehem, he was visited by a young man from Italy. The pilgrim was a great admirer of Jerome and began to lavish praise on the long-forgotten commentary; he even had a copy of it and produced it. Jerome describes the scene pleasantly: "I confess I was astonished that an author, bad as he might be, should find a reader at his own level. He praised me—and I blushed. He lauded to the skies what he called my mystic profundity; and I, with lowered head, dared not confess my shame." Jerome did, in fact, make up for the first failure by publishing a new *Commentary on Obadiah*,[7] the one we possess.

But the best writing he did at Antioch was in his familiar letters. It was then that he actually began correspondence which for the forty-five years that remained was to be the faithful mirror of his life and his thought.

---

7. *Comment. in Abdiam*, Prolog.

PAUL MONCEAUX

In the summer of 375 it was announced in Antioch that Rufinus, who had left Aquileia soon after Jerome, was in Egypt. The news, brought by Heliodorus, was quickly confirmed by others—particularly by a priest of Alexandria who was visiting the Egyptians exiled in Syria for their orthodoxy. Shortly after it was announced that Rufinus was going to Jerusalem with Antonia Melania. The news produced an extraordinary effect upon Jerome. Under the pressure of old memories he spoke of going even to Egypt to find his friend, or at any rate to Jerusalem. But he was a sick man, and he had to rest content with meeting him in imagination: that is, he wrote a letter of rapturous enthusiasm and affection to his friend of the old Roman days, his confrère at Aquileia, Rufinus, who.... But at that time they were still friends.

The letter opened in the tone of the Canticle of Canticles. After the most lyrical salutations and compliments, Jerome went on to say how the news had come to him, and how deeply he regretted that he was tied down by the treason of his wretched body. He told of his journey from Aquileia to Antioch. He spoke of their common friends, Innocentius and Hylas, who had just died; his host Evagrios; above all Bonosus, who had made a final break with his family to live as a hermit on a rock in the Adriatic. And at every point of the letter were protestations of friendship.[8]

---

8. *Epist.* 3.

SAINT JEROME: THE EARLY YEARS

The letter, once written, Jerome was in something of a difficulty. Where should he address it? How get it to a traveller who was rumoured to be on so many different routes? Then someone thought of Florentinus, the Latin monk of Jerusalem to whom Heliodorus owed his recovery. Jerome did not know him personally; but Florentinus was a friend of Evagrios—he was known to be kindness itself; he was so charitable that he had been called "Father of the Poor." Further, he was a man of letters and a collector of books; Jerome was later to levy on his library for the enrichment of his own, offering other books in exchange. For the moment he simply asked him to transmit the letter to Rufinus, thanked him in advance in a charming letter.[9]

If Rufinus received the letter, he seems to have been little moved by all its effusive protestations of friendship. Jerome was already in the desert when he learnt from Florentinus' reply that the friend he had longed for was still in Egypt and gave no signs of life. Jerome took the snub with surprising calmness.[10] It was a first rift in their friendship.

But the important thing, for Jerome's fame and the pleasure of his readers, was that by his charming letters to Rufinus and Florentinus, he had revealed his great gifts as a letter-writer.

---

9. *Epist.* 4, 2.
10. *Epist.* 5, 2.

CHAPTER VI

THE DREAM

WHILE he was lingering on in the great city of Antioch, where obviously he was enjoying himself vastly—too much, perhaps, for one who aspired to be a hermit—Jerome had a strange dream. The account he gives of it—one of his most famous and most original pieces of writing—shows us the state of his soul as he then was—young, scholarly, definitely cast for the ascetical way, but still the Roman rhetorician, too—and makes us see the reason for the direction which, after so many false starts, his life did ultimately take.

Jerome had with him at Antioch the collection of books without which he never travelled. In his long vigils, in the midst of his labours and his austerities, between two prayers or two pieces of work, he would read and re-read Cicero or Virgil, Horace or Plautus.

In the spring of 375, about the middle of Lent, he was seized with a pernicious fever which worked upon him terribly, reducing him to a skeleton, bringing him close to death. One day, he lost consciousness. They thought that he was dead, and began to prepare for his burial.

SAINT JEROME: THE EARLY YEARS

Suddenly, I was rapt in spirit and brought before the tribunal of the Great Judge. There was so much light, such a radiance of glory in those who stood about him, that I fell upon my face, not daring to raise my eyes. I was asked of what condition I was and I answered: "Christian." Then said the Judge: "Thou liest. Thou art a Ciceronian, not a Christian. Where thy treasure is, there is thy heart." Immediately I fell silent. In the midst of the blows (for the Judge had ordered that I be beaten) I was tortured still more by the fire of my conscience. I recalled the verse of the *Psalms*: "In Hell, who shall speak for thee?" Nevertheless I began to cry out, and in my lamentation I said over and over again: "Have pity on me, O Lord, have pity." These words resounded amidst the noise of the rods. At last those who stood by fell at the knees of the Judge. They prayed him to pardon my youth, to permit me to repent of my error, only to chastise me later if in the future I read pagan books. And I, who in so great distress would have promised much beside, made a solemn oath, calling upon the name of God: "Lord, if ever I touch profane books, if I read them, I shall have denied thee."

Upon this oath, I was released and I came once more to the earth. To the surprise of all, I opened my eyes, eyes so bathed in tears that even the hardest of belief must have been convinced of my sorrow. And all that was no mere illusion of sleep, one of those vain dreams which often deceive us. Witness the judgment-seat, before which I lay: witness the sentence, at which I trembled. God grant that I be never subjected to such torments! My shoulders were all bruised, I could still feel the blows after my awakening.[1]

This vivid account was a picture ready made, so that it has inspired many painters, particularly at the end of the Middle Ages and during the Renaissance. Among the works of art which have it for subject, there are two groups. Sometimes the artist simply depicts the scene of the judgment as Jerome describes it. Sometimes the depicting is more complete, in two compartments: the sick man first in bed, then before the dread tribunal.

To the first group belongs a pleasant painting on wood. It is by the Siennese Sano di Pietro and is in the Louvre. In one division of a *predella*, on which are represented different episodes of the life or legend of the saint, we see on the right Jerome, still young, almost naked, bent in an attitude of terror, his back curved under the blows, his head turned

---

1. *Epist.* 22, 30.

SAINT JEROME: THE EARLY YEARS

away: he is being beaten with rods by two angels, before the tribunal of Christ, who is at the left, seated upon a throne and with four personages about him. Among others of the same type is a picturesque scene by Salvator Rosa.

As a specimen of the second group, I shall mention first another painting on wood, also in the Louvre, in the room of the Italian Primitives. On a retable with a *predella* and uprights, attributed to the school of Fra Angelico, and originally in the church of St. Jerome at Fiesole, we see to the left of the Virgin, Jerome holding a book; on the *predella* among scenes from the life and the legend, the story of the dream in two parts. In the left section, Jerome lies on his bed, looking like a corpse, behind the bed a woman keeping vigil, token in hand; in the foreground, their elbows on the valance of the bed, sit a man and woman, overcome with grief. In the section to the right, the Judge, seen full face, sits upon a Throne, with a kind of turban on his head; on either side of the Judge, stand two personages, haloed; before the tribunal is Jerome, on his knees, half naked, beaten with rods by two angels, while two figures, also kneeling, are shown imploring mercy for him.

The same two scenes are to be found on a panel of the Triptych of Bourg-en-Bresse of which I have already spoken. Here they are made mutually dependent, both on the same panel, separated only by an irregular curving line. With an ingenuity which gives proof of an intelligent attention to probability, the artist has relegated to a corner, as it were in the half-light, the supernatural episode of the judgment—an angel scourging Jerome as he kneels before the Judgment seat of Christ, with many figures grouped about. The more ordinary episode of the sick man, on the other hand, is in relief, in high light. Jerome is on the right, lying on a bed, his arms extended, his eyes closed. A woman is coming towards him, holding a dish and a spoon. To the left are two other women; in the background behind the bed, four persons, standing. In the foreground a table, laid with crockery and various utensils; in front of the table, several books lie on the ground, forgotten, stray remnants of the dying man's library.

For the artists, presumably, the Dream has been no more than a tempting subject for a picture. For Jerome himself it was something very different, a definitive event in his life. It impressed him deeply, and his conduct shows its influence. In the years that followed he renounced all profane reading, confining himself to Christian works, studying the Scriptures in particular. He says so explicitly fifteen years later, in a letter of dedication to the two religious, his friends Paula and Eustochium: "You know well," he says, "that for fifteen years my hands have never been lowered towards a Cicero or a Virgil, or any of the pagan authors."[2]

---

2. *Comment. in Epist. ad Galat.*, III, Praefat.

SAINT JEROME: THE EARLY YEARS

But this heroic renunciation made no change in his style; he no longer needed to re-read his favourite classics, since he knew them practically by heart.

But twenty-five years after the Dream, came an old-time friend to call Jerome's sincerity in question. It was the occasion of a curious controversy. In the hottest moment of the battle between the two former friends, Rufinus accused his opponent of having broken his oath never again to read pagan books. To prove his accusation, he instanced the countless classical quotations with which the Abbot of Bethlehem continued to adorn his works, his expositions of pagan authors in the school attached to his monastery, and the classical manuscripts still being copied for him by the monks in Jerusalem.[3] Taken at unawares by this direct attack, Jerome was rather at a loss. He retorted as best he could by arguing from the special facts of the case, objecting that too much importance must not be attached to a dream; that for his dreams no man was responsible; that one could not be bound by an oath taken in sleep; that one's whole life could not be governed by an oath so taken.[4] Obviously, in the years immediately preceding, the pagan authors must have resumed the offensive in his library and in the reading that filled his nights; probably because his

---

3. Rufinus, *Apologia contra Hieronymum*, II, 6.
4. Jerome, *Apologia contra Rufinum*, I, 30–31; III, 32.

memory was now less faithful. But that is no reason why we should suspect either the sincerity or the strength of the resolutions he took immediately after the dream.[5] A holy man is a man; and a man sometimes changes his mind in twenty-five years.

What is more extraordinary is that in our own day certain critics have challenged the actual occurrence of the dream, dismissing it as a mere rhetorical device. Endless ingenuity has been wasted in the hunt for analogies between Jerome's story and other stories, Greek and Latin, pagan and Christian. The analogies are beside the point, proving nothing against Jerome's sincerity or the reality of the dream. Visions and dreams of this sort, which always haunted the imagination of the ancients, had still more power over the minds of Christians, precisely as they believed more firmly in the Last Judgment. What is significant in Jerome's story, what constitutes its psychological value, is neither the dream itself, nor the setting, nor the judgment seat of God; but the matter of the indictment and the sentence; the prohibition against the reading of pagan authors. This was something altogether new in literature of the kind. It is in this that Jerome's story is original and illuminating; it brings marvellously into light the painful conflict then tormenting the young man, torn between the

---

5. *Epist.* 22, 3.

SAINT JEROME: THE EARLY YEARS

exigencies of his Christian asceticism and the habits—now second nature—of the scholar unashamed, the rhetorician fashioned in the schools.

The proof that Jerome was sincere in his narration of a real dream is that he went off to the desert.

CHAPTER VII

ENTRY INTO THE DESERT

THE impression made upon his mind by the Dream, by the oath he had uttered before the mysterious tribunal, led Jerome to a re-examination of his past life. In his disturbed imagination, with a sort of holy fear that was very close to remorse, he lived over again his vocation at Treves, the resolutions made at Aquileia, his setting out as a pilgrim, his long journeying over Thrace and Asia Minor, his eye fixed upon Jerusalem. It had been his design first to kneel in the holy city upon all the spots hallowed by the steps of the Saviour, then to go into utter seclusion in some cell or cavern. His strength had failed him before the completion of his pilgrimage: he had had to give up Jerusalem. Now it came over him with a shock that for a year he had lingered mindless of his vocation amidst the delights of Antioch, hard alongside the waiting desert.

In truth he had never abandoned his design; as witness the letter he wrote, towards the end of 374, to a community of monks governed by a certain Theodosius, probably the abbot Theodosius, spoken of by the historian Theodoret,

SAINT JEROME: THE EARLY YEARS

who had founded the monastery of Rhosos in the north of Syria, near the frontier of Cilicia.[1] Jerome had received hospitality in this pious house and he retained a glowing memory of it. He wrote to his hosts of a day to thank them; after a wistful regret for their "paradise," for their "desert more charming than any tower," he asked them to obtain by their prayers that God should grant him the strength to make final renunciation of the world, to live like them in solitude.[2]

The breakdown of his health, grave illness, then the studies and the works he had undertaken, the lectures of Apollinaris, the enchantment of Antioch—all caused him to postpone from one month to the next, the carrying-out of his design. Many times he reproached himself. In his letter to Rufinus, at the end of an excited panegyric of Bonosus, won by him to asceticism and become a hermit before him, there broke from him the cry of distress: "Pardon me, O Christ, for having been unable to keep my promise."[3]

If he had faltered, it was through no fear of the desert, nor of the renunciation and austerity of the hermit's life. In the solitude of the desert, the one thing he dreaded was solitude of the heart. He could not bring himself to do without friendship for evermore, so he dreamed of taking a friend with him.

---

1. Theodoret, *Hist. Relig.* 10.
2. *Epist.* 2.
3. *Epist.* 3, 5.

Then Heliodorus arrived from Jerusalem. This was the companion of his dreams. To bear him off, Jerome made lavish use of all his gifts. With his usual tenacity, with all the arts of diplomacy and every resource of a wise strategy, he laid siege month after month to this God-sent friend.

When he had left Aquileia for Jerusalem, Heliodorus had probably given more than a hint that he meant to go off and live with Jerome in the desert.[4] But once in the East, his vocation wavered. He had not borne easily the fatigues of the journey; he had been seriously ill in Jerusalem.[5] When he left the Holy City his one idea was to go home. But he went by Antioch. There he found Jerome, and Jerome did everything possible to win him back to their original idea.

There were lengthy arguments, incessant and daily renewed, between the two friends. Heliodorus was not renouncing asceticism. But for a Christian there were then very various ways of practising it: the solitary life of the hermits, life in community in a monastery under a rule, free communities of pious men, ascetics living in the world like the *continentes* of earlier generations. Heliodorus, though he had not yet said so, and even perhaps did not yet know it, had already made his choice.

---

4. *Ego et Heliodorus carissimus pariter habitare solitudinem Syriae Chalcidis nitebamur* (*Comment. in Abdiam*, Prolog.).
5. *Epist.* 4, 1.

SAINT JEROME: THE EARLY YEARS

In vain did Jerome, with his colourful eloquence, vaunt the superiority of the anchorite's life, wherein a man might pray or meditate day and night, and work at his will, far from the noise and the distractions of the world. Heliodorus did not deny it, but he hesitated, multiplying objections. Less original than Jerome, of less personality, slow-moving, matter-of-fact, without imagination, without passion, he saw things with a different eye. The desert did not attract him; solitude sounded frightening. He told himself that a man could save his soul equally well in the world. Then he thought of his native land, his family and his friends in Altinum. Had he any right to abandon his father, his mother, his widowed sister, a small nephew whose support and guide he was? He thought also of the household slaves, practically his comrades, of the worthy souls who had reared him and loved him—his old nurse, his foster-father.[6] He would not say yes and dared not say no. He could not decide, quietly evaded the issue, fearing to offend a friend, but fearing also to embark lightly on so difficult a way. And the months passed and the desert was still waiting.

At last, as Jerome was losing patience and threatening to go off by himself, Heliodorus screwed up his courage. He declared that they should see later. For the moment he

---

6. *Epist.* 14, 2–3.

must return to his country; he wanted to see his people again, rebuild his health, put his affairs in order. In this way, too, he would be able to profit by the experience his friend had gained; Jerome would write to him from the desert would tell him quite frankly his impressions, and would then by his eloquence vanquish his friend's last hesitations and scruples.[7]

When Heliodorus left Antioch for Upper Italy the two friends parted in tears, with promises of eternal affection.[8] Jerome had to be resigned. From his desert he wrote Heliodorus an enthusiastic letter; he was eloquent, urgent, charming.[9] But Heliodorus did not return. Soon came the news that he was a priest; soon after, that he was Bishop of Altinum. Miraculously, Jerome forgave; in fact redoubled his attentions to the deserter, extending his affection even to the nephew, the small Nepotianus who had been part cause of the desertion.[10]

That he should have forgiven him so completely is the most staggering proof of the depth of his friendship for Heliodorus. Having seen the fugitive as far as the gates of Antioch, Jerome made up his mind to go to the desert alone. With his bodily illnesses, his intellectual curiosity, the siege

---

7. *Epist.* 14, 1.
8. *Epist.* 6, 2; 9; 14, 1.
9. *Epist.* 14.
10. *Epist.* 52 and 60.

SAINT JEROME: THE EARLY YEARS

he had laid to his friend, it had been a long wavering. Now he was once more master of himself. The decision made, he felt calmer, almost happy. He set off, young in heart, full of enthusiasm, of boyish faith and of illusions.

The desert would probably have made a permanent conquest of him, if it had not been peopled with bellicose monks.

PART III

§

THE DESERT

INTRODUCTORY

At the moment of Jerome's entry into the Syrian desert he fully believed that he would never leave it. He was barely twenty-eight, but he had broken resolutely with the world. If henceforth he was to have communication with men, it should be only under pressure of actual needs—the material needs of a life of privations close to nature, and the intellectual and moral needs of a literary hermit who had renounced all things save study and the friendship of men. With a mind only for salvation, he should live henceforth for naught but prayer, meditation and labour. Gazing down these vistas, he foresaw an infinity of joy. In these desolate solitudes he would savour some foretaste of the happiness of the elect.

Alas, he reckoned without certain realities—the failures of his poor body, the offensives to be launched by the

PAUL MONCEAUX

World and the Devil, the phantoms wherewith imagination peopled his solitude, the sullen or even brutal hostility of the monks who belonged there—troublesome neighbours, over-inquisitive and cross-grained, armed against him as an intruder. After the lyric enthusiasm of his first entry, he was to come down to earth. Two years and a half later, ill, embittered, disillusioned, he left his desert amidst a storm of mutual abuse.

CHAPTER I

JEROME'S CAVE IN THE DESERT

THE desert of his choice was known at that time as the Desert of Chalcis.¹ It was a corner of the great desert of Syria, which, to the west of Mesopotamia, extended from the loop of the Euphrates to the borders of Arabia.

The town of Chalcis, today Kinnesrîn (the eagle's nest), or Eski-Haleb (old Aleppo), was fifty-three miles to the south-east of Antioch, eighteen miles to the south of Beroea (Aleppo). It was a Greek city, founded three centuries before Christ by King Seleucos Nicator, on the bank of a small stream on the site of an ancient native village. To distinguish it from the Chalcis in Lebanon it had been surnamed Chalcis *ad Belum*.²

It was on the caravan route from Antioch to the middle valley of the Euphrates. There, too, the road from Cyrrhos to Emesa crossed the old road from Antioch to Beroea, of which sections have been found. Thanks to this situation,

---

1. Jerome, *Vita Malchi*, 3: *Ad eremum Chalcidos*, cf. *Epist.* 5, 1; 7, 1.
2. See the review *Syria* (1925), pp. 339ff.

the town had prospered. It occupied the centre of a vast rolling plain, called after it the Chilcidian and held to be the most fertile region of Syria.

In the wars between the Seleucids and the Arabs it played an important part, and later in the wars of the Byzantines against the Persians. Conquered by the Arabs in 629, it was for some time, under their dominion, the capital of Northern Syria. It had then a new period of prosperity. But it began to decline when the caravan route turned aside from it. Gradually it was abandoned by its inhabitants, who went to Aleppo. From the thirteenth century it has been practically deserted.

In Jerome's time Chalcis was a town of some importance, enriched by agriculture and by commerce. It was surrounded by walls, built for its protection against sudden attacks by the nomads of the desert, the dreaded Saracens. A Greek inscription has been discovered, once built into the wall near one of the city gates. It is a metrical dedication, in bad iambic trimeters, informing us that above the gates had been placed an image of the Christ the Saviour, with portraits of authorities—emperors, prefects of the Praetorium, the bishop of the city Jerome's cave in the desert and others. Protected by these powerful patrons, the town declared its defiance of "barbarian incursions."[3]

---

3. Waddington, *Inscriptions de Syrie*, n. 1,832.

SAINT JEROME: THE EARLY YEARS

This naive confidence had no effect upon the course of events; the inscription and the images did not succeed in intimidating Persians, or Saracens, or Arabs, or Turks. About 542, threatened with pillage by Chosroes, king of Persia, Chalcis was forced to save itself by a heavy ransom. Again, in 550, the emperor Justinian ordered the town to restore its fortifications or to rebuild and complete them. To these works (mentioned by Procopius), which were directed by the celebrated engineer Isidore of Miletus, relate two other Greek inscriptions, likewise built into the city wall.

Today at Kinnesrîn are still to be seen quite considerable remains of these walls, with the basements of the towers. In the lower town, as on the acropolis, traces of streets can be distinguished, bordered by ruins of houses or monuments. To the north of the city, on the slopes of a rocky hill, stretches a vast necropolis with tombs in the earth and well-preserved sepulchral vaults.

Not far from the walls of Chalcis, a few miles to the south and east, began the desert, stretching away to Palmyra and beyond—a desert of broken ground and great variety of aspect, where sterile valleys—sometimes arid, sometimes marshy—ran between rocky cliffs wherein were caves which had doubtless sheltered generations of troglodytes. To this place came Jerome in search of the solitude of his dreams. It was a shock to find the solitude overpopulated. The deserts of Syria were already thronged with hermits. Egypt had shown the way. As long before, under the Pharaohs and the Ptolemys, the devotions of Egypt had overflowed and flooded the adjacent lands.

The first generations of Christians had known practically no other types of ascetic than the *continentes* and the consecrated virgins, seeking to realise the evangelical ideal, but without separation from the world, content to occupy a place of honour in the communities. Towards the end of the third century and the beginning of the fourth, Egypt inaugurated two new forms of asceticism: first, with St. Anthony, the life of the hermit; a little later, with St. Pachomius, monasticism, life in community in monasteries living under a rule and sometimes affiliated to a large congregation.

Everyone knows the splendid literary and artistic flowering of legends concerning St. Anthony—especially his Temptations, a theme which fascinated Flaubert and has cast its spell over so many painters. Before becoming a figure of legend St. Anthony was a very real person: he is vigorously alive in the accounts of his biographers, in the Greek narrative of his friend Athanasius, and in the Latin adaptation made by Evagrios of Antioch, Jerome's host. This prototype of all hermits was a true peasant of Egypt: a dreamer, headstrong, totally illiterate, with an equal loathing for society and the alphabet. For over eighty years he lived as a solitary ascetic; at first outside his own house,

SAINT JEROME: THE EARLY YEARS

which he had sold, then in a tomb, then in the Arabian desert in the ruins of a fortress, finally under the palms of an oasis near the Red Sea. His ruling idea was to be alone; for that he was always ready to move house, in flight alike from admirers and the merely curious, in flight even from his disciples. He gained his bread by making mats, and lived only for prayer, fasting, reverie—despite the demons who strove relentlessly against him in his solitude. Only twice did he leave his desert; both times he went to Alexandria. During Diocletian's persecution he went there in search of martyrdom; later he went to greet the bishop, Athanasius, returning from exile, and he battled there against the Arians. He died in 356, aged one hundred and five, bequeathing to Athanasius all he possessed—the old cloak that was his bed, and his sheep-skin tunic. In his own despite he had become famous. He had many disciples, most of them living solitary like himself, without head or rule. He remained the model of all anchorites.

From Egypt the new asceticism rapidly gained the other coast of the Red Sea and the peninsula of Sinai. In the gorges and on the slopes of the sacred mountain many hermits set up their dwelling. Like the nomads of the region, they made the little town of Pharan their centre. Their imaginations stirred by memory of Biblical incidents, these solitaries thought they had located the precise situation of the scenes of Exodus, thus fixing the topography of Sinai in that regard. A chapel arose on the summit of Djebel Mousa, the mountain of Moses; an oratory, marking the place of the burning bush, on Djebel Katarin—where today we visit the monastery of St. Catherine. Other chapels and hermitages were to be found in the lonely places of the littoral. But the hermits there did not always find peace any more than their brethren of the mountain. Despite their poverty, they excited the cupidity of the barbarians round about them, the pirates of the Red Sea and the Bedouins of the interior, who often in the course of their *razzias* captured them to sell them as slaves or immolate them to their idols.

In Phoenicia, where the population remained for the most part pagan, hermits were comparatively rare. Among them are mentioned two disciples of St. Anthony: Cronios and James the Cripple. In Palestine, Egyptian asceticism was introduced by Hilarion. He, too, was St. Anthony's disciple, having visited him in the desert. Back in his own country, he, with a few companions, had inaugurated the eremitical life, on an arid foreshore to the south of Gaza. He had thousands of disciples who flowed over into the desert places of Palestine and even close up to Jerusalem, where from one hermitage to another all tongues were to be heard.

Syria and Mesopotamia were conquered in their turn. The oldest of the solitaries of these regions was Aones, who had settled near Harran, by the well where Jacob and

SAINT JEROME: THE EARLY YEARS

Rachel had met. Gradually hermitages and chapels grew up about the places consecrated by the memory of Abraham, Rebecca, Moses, Elijah. Colonies of hermits were set up around Edessa and Antioch. In spite of the ever-present menace of Saracen raids, the deserts of Syria were thronged with solitaries—to the southeast of Chalcis, round Palmyra, and in many places besides. These Syrian hermits were already renowned for the unusualness of their austerities, which sometimes reached eccentricity. Some affected to live like the beasts, eating only uncooked herbs. Others had themselves attached to a rock by chains embedded in it. Later came a wave of "stylites," who wished to come nearer heaven by spending their lives on a pillar. Jerome saw with his own eyes certain eccentricities in the desert of Chalcis, and he has left us details. One man had lodged in an old cistern where, that he might not die too soon of hunger, he ate a total of five figs a day. Another never left his cave in thirty years, living on barley bread and muddy water.[4]

The spot chosen by Jerome, between the cultivated region of Syria and the lands of the nomad Saracen, must have been near the town of Chalcis with its fortification, behind which the hermits might take refuge in case of attack. It was not very far from Antioch, so that Jerome's

---

4. *Vita Pauli*, 6.

friends could visit him and, at least from time to time, bring him his post.

As to the material conditions of his life in the desert, he gives us no explicit information. What is certain is that he was not living in a monastery, as some of his biographers seem to think. He never makes the faintest allusion to this supposed monastery. All that he tells us absolutely excludes this hypothesis. Certainly he sometimes speaks of his *cellula* in the desert, but by that word he means simply "an ascetic's dwelling," and one of the texts in question proves that this *cellula* was a cave.[5] From what he says of that time, we must conclude that he really led the life of a hermit, that he lived alone and was not under any superior or any rule. But he had neighbours, other hermits, who were sometimes very troublesome. Note, too, that his dwelling must have been fairly spacious and comparatively comfortable, since he could lodge his library in it, and not only work in it himself but have youthful copyists working under his eye.[6]

If we would picture the externals of his life, it is sufficient to recall the colonies of hermits of the Egyptian desert of Nitria, whose organisation was taken as a model. To the south-west of Alexandria, in a desolate region, stretched the gloomy "valley of nitre," with its salt lakes and its double

---

5. *Epist.* 17, 2; cf. *Epist.* 22, 7.
6. *Epist.* 5, 2.

SAINT JEROME: THE EARLY YEARS

border of rugged cliffs. It extended, growing ever wilder, through the rocks of the Desert of Cells and the sands of the Desert of Scete. There from the middle of the fourth century, hermits had ventured forth and multiplied, widely different in origin and condition. These hermits lived in caves or huts, sometimes alone, sometimes in groups of two or three. Free of all duty, without rule or superior, they passed their time as they chose—praying, meditating, chanting psalms, reading or sleeping, their hands usually occupied in basket-making. Saturday and Sunday, most of them met in the centre of the valley, to attend religious ceremonies in a church served by priests subject to the bishop of Hermopolis. In front of the church were three palm trees. From each of these trees hung a whip, meant for the punishment of evildoers, but often used by the hermits to chastise themselves for their faults or to accelerate their moral progress.[7]

In some such external framework we may imagine the colony of hermits in the desert of Chalcis. They lived singly or in groups at their choice, but without being able to cut themselves off completely from their neighbours. They had to have their church, dependent upon the bishop of Chalcis, served probably by the priest Marcus who was in correspondence with Jerome and who sought to keep—or

---

7. Palladios, *Lausiac History*, VII, 3.

re-establish—peace in the valley.[8] As to the cell in which Jerome dwelt, it was simply—as in the Egyptian desert called the Desert of Cells—a natural cave more or less made fit for habitation. He himself wrote at the time, concerning the monks of the desert of Chalcis: "From the caverns of our cells—*de cavernis cellularum*—we condemn the world."[9] Those artists have seen aright who have so often depicted Jerome praying, meditating, reading, writing, in a cave or in front of a cave in the desert.

---

8. *Epist.* 17.
9. *Epist.* 17, 2.

CHAPTER II

HYMN TO THE DESERT

LAND and sky, the transparence of the atmosphere, rock, sands, closeness to nature, the beasts, solitude and the distant echoes of human societies—everything in the desert of Chalcis enchanted Jerome at first. His enthusiasm burst forth in his letters, in which he declared with verve that he had found the retreat of his dreams. In the very first words of his first letter, he proudly sets down his new address—"in that part of the desert which, near to Syria, adjoins the land of the Saracens."[1]

One day, wishing to attract one of his dearest friends, that Heliodorus of whom we have heard, he intoned in honour of the desert a lyric hymn, a hymn by turns grandiose and intimate, which he compared to a song of sailors coming into port: "O desert new-springing with the flowers of Christ! O solitude, wherein are born those stones of which, as the Apocalypse tells, the city is built of the great King! O place of hermits rejoicing in the close friendship of

---

1. *Epist.* 5, 1; cf. *Epist.* 7, 1.

God! What dost thou, brother, in the world, who art greater than the world? How long shall the shadows of roofs oppress thee? How long shall the smoky prison of the cities enclose thee? The light I look upon, believe me, is strangely brighter. Here it is my joy to shake off the burden of flesh and fly up to the pure radiance of heaven..."[2]

Truly Jerome, many a century before Fromentin and Loti, felt the poetry of the desert. But what, more than all, he sought there, and found, was the radiation of the divine, the more intimate communion with God. These desolate solitudes, through which ran the strait way of salvation, were for him like an earthly dependency, far off and wild, of Paradise.

Upon his arrival he drew up, and to the end he followed like the most scrupulous of St. Anthony's disciples, a programme governing his life as hermit. He slept on the bare ground. He wore a garment made of the coarsest sackcloth. As was the custom of the hermits, he abandoned all care of the body; his skin, he says, became rough and dirty, like an Ethiopian's. He practically lived on bread and water, sometimes adding some fruit or a raw vegetable, but never anything cooked. His health was delicate and was extremely ill-suited by this regime—quite apart from the fact that he was by nature something of a gourmand and

---

2. *Epist.* 14, 10.

SAINT JEROME: THE EARLY YEARS

had always appreciated good food. For all that, he fasted frequently and sometimes prolonged his fasting for weeks together. To such a point did he push his thirst for privations that he more and more undermined his poor body, already so feeble. He had at that time the pallor that goes with sick men and with ascetics who abuse austerity. He had grown so thin, he says, that his bones, scarcely hanging together, drove into each other.[3]

Like the anchorites of Egypt, he had to give himself to some manual occupation. He tells us, indeed, that by his labour he earned his daily bread: "I have robbed no one," he writes: "I am no idler in receipt of charity. By our arms, in the sweat of our brow, we gain our food each day." We know that the Apostle has written: "If a man will not work, neither let him eat."[4] Jerome was not the man to be afraid of any work whatever.

In these first days of his dwelling in the desert, the one thing from which he sometimes suffered was his isolation, his moral solitariness. He had neighbours, but no one near to whom he could open his soul. Most often, indeed, as he did not understand the Aramaic dialects in use in that region, he was condemned either to silence or monologue. He wrote to his friends at Aquileia: "Your letters are the

---

3. *Epist.* 17, 2.
4. *Epist.* 22, 7.

only things here that know Latin. I must either learn a barbarous tongue or else keep silent."[5] Keeping silence must have been the cruellest trial for an orator—at any rate this orator—pupil of the rhetoricians, who in the long past at Rome had made so joyous a companion, and who lately at Antioch had charmed his friends by the freshness and brilliance of his conversation.

He consoled himself for the silence by study, the only one of this world's joys he had not renounced. He read, read without ceasing, night and day. Naturally he had brought his library, begun at Rome and steadily added to since, which always travelled with him. If after his famous dream he denied himself the reading of the classics, he made up for it with Scripture and Christian literature. "Thanks to the Lord," he wrote, "we have here in abundance manuscripts of the sacred books."[6] But there were gaps in other fields—exegesis, literature, history, and the filling of these gaps was one of his principal occupations and preoccupations in the desert.

Since he could not himself transcribe all the manuscripts, he had formed a team of helpers; quite young men, *alumni*, foundlings gathered up by Christian charity. He had presumably brought them from Antioch, and he had taught

---

5. *Epist.* 7, 2.
6. *Epist.* 5, 2.

SAINT JEROME: THE EARLY YEARS

them the art of copying. He had them working under his surveillance, not for his library only, but also for his friends and perhaps for others; thereby, we may assume, gaining funds for the keep and payment of his band.[7] To furnish occupation for his copyists, he approached his friends with requests that they lend him manuscripts or send him copies.

His correspondence contains some interesting sidelights on this. It had been announced that Rufinus was coming at once to Jerusalem, and as Rufinus was well provided with books, Jerome wished to take advantage of the opportunity. So he begged Florentinus, who lived in Jerusalem, to take the necessary steps to obtain copies of various works possessed by their common friend: the Commentary of Reticius of Autun on the Canticle of Canticles, several books of Tertullian, the *Synodes* of Hilary of Poitiers and his *Commentary on the Psalms*. In return if Florentinus wished, they in the desert would transcribe for him the Scriptural books he lacked, probably the Latin text.[8] Later on, Paul of Concordia, the centenarian collector of books, received a request of the same sort: in spite of the distance, Jerome asked him to send the *Commentaries on the Gospels* of Fortunatianus of Aquileia, Aurelius Victor's *History*, the *Letters* of Novatian.[9] Of these three authors, the first was

---

7. *Habeo alumnos, qui antiquariae arti serviant* (ibid.).
8. *Epist.* 5, 2.
9. *Epist.* 10, 3.

an Arian, the second a pagan, the third a schismatic. The hermit's library was not narrow-minded.

While adding to his library, Jerome was adding likewise to his equipment of scholarship.

The Greek of the New Testament was familiar to him but he was hampered by his inability to read the Old Testament in the original text. He decided therefore to learn Hebrew, with the aid of a converted Jew, probably a hermit living near. This study he at first found so forbidding that it was a real mortification. Thirty years later he still remembered it: "When I was young and living alone behind the rampart of the desert I had no strength against the allurement of vices and the heat of nature. In vain did I multiply fasts to break this yoke; my imagination boiled in the fire of sinful thoughts. To conquer it I put myself under the direction of a certain brother, a converted Jew. After the subtlety of Quintilian, the flowing eloquence of Cicero, the gravity of Fronto, the charms of Pliny, I was learning an alphabet, striving to pronounce words that hissed and panted. What pain I bore! What difficulties! How often I despaired! How often I gave up, to begin again in my obstinate wish to learn."[10] His obstinacy was rewarded by success. Upon his return to Rome he could teach Hebrew to Paula and her daughters, and he never ceased to deepen his knowledge

---

10. *Epist.* 125, 12.

SAINT JEROME: THE EARLY YEARS

of the language. After he had settled in Bethlehem, he put himself under the tuition of another Jew, Baranina, whose lessons were expensive—and always given at night, for fear of his fellow Jews.[11] Thanks to this long and fruitful labour, he became a master in the field: his Latin translation of the Old Testament from the Hebrew became the Vulgate for the Universal Church.

Such were Jerome's occupations in the desert; to them we must add the writing of letters and of a charming piece of hagiography in which he revealed all his talent. This original existence—a hermit who was at the same time scholar, collector of books and writer—vividly struck the imagination first of his contemporaries, later of many artists. From that came a whole cycle of pictures. Between the fourteenth and the eighteenth century they were so numerous that today our museums are thronged with them. Leaving aside for the moment the pictures of Jerome as Penitent, which will be mentioned later, they are to be grouped under five different themes, of each of which I shall quote a few examples.

(1) *Jerome among the Hermits.* Of this scene, rarely depicted, there is a specimen in Rome, in the Church of Santa Maria degli Angeli. It is a painting by Muziano, with landscape by Bril.

---

11. *Epist.* 84, 3.

PAUL MONCEAUX

(2) *Jerome at Prayer.* In the Louvre, in the Room of the Italian Primitives, an anonymous picture on wood, shows the Saint kneeling outside his cave; near him is the lion.

At Frankfurt on Main, a painting by Gerard David shows Jerome at prayer, kneeling before a tree from which hangs a little picture of Christ on the cross between the Virgin and St. John; lion and rocks in the background.

The scene is more complex in a composition by Paul Bril in the Louvre. To the left in a hollow gorge between enormous rocks, at the entry of a cave, Jerome at prayer, kneeling before a crucifix; nearby, the lion; further off, two men, one mounted on an ass; to the right, two shepherds, goats, sheep.

(3) *Jerome in Meditation.* There is a picture in the National Gallery, London, by Bono da Ferrara; between two very high rocks, a gorge, at the far end of which one sees other rocks and the corner of a monastery; in the foreground sits Jerome in monastic dress, meditating; at his feet, the lion; there are books behind him.

In the Louvre is a picture by Giovanni Dosso; the saint lies before his cave, wrapt in thought, gazing upon a crucifix; on the right lies the lion; background of mountains.

(4) *Jerome Reading.* In the Benson Collection, in London, is a charming picture by Giovanni Bellini; a scene of trees and great rocks; in the foreground, near a pond with reeds, sits Jerome, book in hand.

SAINT JEROME: THE EARLY YEARS

In the National Gallery there is a picture by Basaiti; the Saint in the desert, sitting on a rock, reading a book that rests on his left knee; some buildings partly showing among crags.

By the same artist, a painting in the Kaufmann Collection in Berlin; in a scene like the other, Jerome meditates, a book on his knees; half-lying on the edge of a slope, he is resting on his right arm, his hand under his head; further back, the lion.

(5) *Jerome at Work.* The most characteristic specimen is in Madrid, a curious and powerful picture by Ribera. Jerome is shown at the entrance of a cave, seated, with his back against a rock. He is bald, emaciated, his features drawn painfully. In the left hand he holds a roll of paper, the end of which, covered with writing, is spread on his knees. In his outstretched right arm is a pen, and he is writing on a leaf of papyrus, set down flat on some great stones near the enormous head of a placid lion. Behind the Saint, other books, surmounted by a skull. To the left, through the opening of the cave, one sees a fragment of desolate country.

In most of the paintings just mentioned and in many similar two anachronisms stand out. The young hermit—he was twenty-eight to thirty, remember—becomes an old man at the end of his strength; and he is given as companion in the desert that lion which literary tradition associates, not with the desert, but with the abbot long after in Bethlehem.

PAUL MONCEAUX

These two errors both have as their chief source the confusion between Jerome's two periods in the East. In the accounts he gives of his time as a hermit Jerome repeatedly says that he was then young, but in vain; erroneously people have attributed to age the weaknesses which were really the result of ill health. As to the lion, which in the Middle Ages had become the symbol of the Saint, it was perhaps natural that they should restore it to the desert whence it must obviously have come.

In a picture by Bordone, at the Musée de l'Ermitage, there is a kind of compromise between the artistic and literary traditions. The picture shows the arrival of the lion, but in conditions very different from those popularised by the legend. Jerome is in the desert, but close to a monastery, which is seen in the background. Sitting on a huge stone before a book and a crucifix, he is turning towards the lion which is climbing the rocky platform, with only its head and forepaws showing. It would almost seem as though the painter wished to justify the artistic tradition by transposing the scene!

At any rate, if we pass condemnation on the twofold anachronism we must admit that many artists, in their efforts to recreate Jerome in his desert, have attained a degree of probability not too far removed from the reality of history.

CHAPTER III

LETTERS FROM THE DESERT

JEROME had always had a passion for friendship equal to his passion for study. In the desert, solitude intensified and sometimes made almost unbearable his longing for distant friends, his desire to share in their lives, at least in thought, the necessity he felt of opening his soul to them, his fear that they might forget him. In all that time he was a most industrious correspondent—so industrious that he sometimes complained of shortage of paper, compelling him to be too brief or to pack his lines too close.[1] Among the many letters he wrote from the desert a dozen have survived. In them, though without any such design, the youthful hermit paints his whole self, with his enthusiasms and his moments of gloom, his controversial ardour, his intellectual curiosity and his mystical hopes, his cult of friendship—and all the refinements, hurt feelings and resentments of his too exacting affection.

---

1. *Epist.* 11.

PAUL MONCEAUX

His letters went by Antioch. Evagrios, who paid him frequent visits, brought or sent him his post, and forwarded his replies, so serving as point of contact between the hermit and his friends of East and West.[2] These visits of Evagrios were an enchantment to the solitary, but pleasure in his coming was followed inevitably by the melancholy of his going, rendering the solitude doubly cruel.[3]

Jerome was barely settled in the desert when he received two letters that delighted him—one from the far end of the Adriatic, the other from Jerusalem.

In the first, his old friend Paul of Concordia made pleasant mention of the past and asked him to get back his manuscript of Tertullian, which Rufinus, having borrowed it and carried it off to the East, had, apparently, no idea of returning. Jerome at once passed on the request.[4]

Shortly after, he remembered that Paul was entering upon his hundredth year. Upon this he wrote him a charming letter, congratulating him enthusiastically on his green old age. For his feast he sent his portrait! "Now the circle of your hundredth year revolves for you; and you, ever faithful to the commands of the Lord, prepare for the joys of the life to come by those of the present life. Your

---

2. *Epist.* 7, 1; 15, 5.
3. *Epist.* 7, 1.
4. *Epist.* 5, 2.

SAINT JEROME: THE EARLY YEARS

eyes preserve all their brilliance; your step is firm; your hearing is acute, your teeth white, your voice musical, your body vigorous and full of sap; the white of your hair contrasts with the red of your skin. Your strength belies your age. Your sureness of memory is not diminished as it usually is in advanced age. Your blood does not flow colder, to dim and chill the mind. There is no wrinkling of the face beneath a furrowed brow. Your hand does not tremble, letting the pen-point wander over the wax in uncertain lines. In you the Lord shows all the splendour of our future resurrection..."[5] Such a centenarian might well be the envy of many of his juniors.

The letter from Jerusalem was Florentinus' reply to Jerome's letter from Antioch; it informed him that Rufinus stayed on in Egypt and gave no news of himself. Jerome wrote at once to thank his correspondent. He regretted more than ever, he said, that he had been unable to go as far as Jerusalem; at least he would like to keep up a regular correspondence with his new friend. If he must now be resigned to seeing Rufinus no more, he would yet wish to obtain from him copies of certain works. If Florentinus would act as intermediary in this matter, he would send him in return the scriptural books he lacked.[6]

---

5. *Epist.* 10, 2.
6. *Epist.* 5, 1–2.

The postscript is rather surprising in a letter from a hermit to a monk. Florentinus wanted to recover one of his slaves who had fled and was now in Antioch with a *plagiator*—a receiver—and Jerome said he had asked Evagrios to follow the matter up.

But Jerome's principal correspondence from the desert was with his compatriots of the Aquileia region. The more he felt the distance between himself and them, the more joy he found in being with them in spirit. As it happens, his letters of that period vary so much in tone that we can measure the degrees of his feeling for each at the moment. They show in the clearest light what a passion he had for friendship and how exigent was his affection. He was himself most regular in his correspondence, and he made no allowance for any failure in this regard. If he rejoiced in the slightest letter that came from a friend in Aquileia or the neighbouring cities, he noted with mistrust and anxiety the long silences of the less regular, silences into which his impatient imagination read a falling-off in friendship.

Upon those who had written of their own motion he lavished the most moving expressions of gratitude, full of lyric effusions and touching words. Replying to his friend Julianus, deacon of Aquileia, he amusingly threatened so to overwhelm him with letters that he would beg for mercy. Since he had no news from his family or his native town, since he held in special disdain the bites of the "Spanish

SAINT JEROME: THE EARLY YEARS

viper" (probably Bishop Lupicinus), he was all the more grateful to Julianus, who had informed him of his sister's progress in the ascetical life. He begged the deacon, who was the girl's spiritual director, to keep him informed.[7]

From three other friends of Aquileia, the priest Chromatius, his brother Eusebius and the archdeacon Jovinus, Jerome had received a collective letter, asking for news of himself and telling him of the heroic decision of Bonosus, who had become a hermit on an islet in the Adriatic. Jerome began his reply by mentioning with some circumstance that he, too, was living in a desert, whither his friends' letter had been sent him by the kindness of Evagrios. This letter, he added, had caused him intense joy. He had read and re-read it. It was all the dearer to him because it spoke Latin in the midst of barbarians, brought before his eyes the faces of his one-time companions, made him feel as though he were conversing with them.[8]

After an enthusiastic panegyric of Bonosus and the eremitical life,[9] Jerome asked his friends to watch over his sister, to assist the deacon Julianus in his task of director, to obtain that Valerianus himself, the Bishop of Aquileia, should write to the girl for her encouragement.[10] She had the more

---

7. *Epist.* 6.
8. *Epist.* 7, 1–2.
9. *Epist.* 7, 3.
10. *Epist.* 7, 4.

need of their counsels in that she could find no help in her own city, by reason of the ignorance of the Christians of Stridon and their bishop, Lupicinus.[11] This railing note and the rancour it betrays stood in strong contrast to his touching salutations to the mother and sisters of Chromatius, his almost lyrical eulogy of that holy house where all lived as ascetics, where to the virtues were added the glory of martyrdom through their struggle against the Arian heresy.[12]

The tone was colder, dryer, in his letters to old friends who seemed to have forgotten him. Niceas, sub-deacon of Aquileia, whom he had seen but lately in Antioch, gave no sign of life since his return to the West; with much reinforcement of erudite quotations, Jerome called upon him to write, even if he believed he had some cause of complaint.[13] There are similar reproaches to the monk Chrysocomas, with this sally: "Perhaps you will say you had nothing to write. Very well! You should have written to say you had nothing to write."[14]

Luckless, indeed, were those of his compatriots who had not answered his letters. These he addressed almost as enemies, rebuking them resentfully and almost arrogantly, with bitter allusions to the calumnies which had forced him

---

11. *Epist.* 7, 5.
12. *Epist.* 7, 6.
13. *Epist.* 9.
14. *Epist.* 8.

SAINT JEROME: THE EARLY YEARS

to leave his country and were still vigorous against him, with protestations of innocence and passionate appeals to the judgment of God.

To the consecrated virgins of Hemona, he had written many times, without obtaining a word in reply. In the letter that has survived he was very near to anger; at least he read a lesson to those holy women. Perhaps they despised him for past errors—a Pharisaical severity to which he opposed our Lord's kindness. He took a loftier tone as he protested against the merely human injustice. He warned the religious against the calumnies of his adversaries. "The hateful judgment of men, my very dear sisters, is one thing, the judgment of Christ another. At His judgment seat is not pronounced the same sentence as in the corners where slanderers whisper."[15]

In the same town of Hemona lived the monk Antonius, who likewise turned a deaf ear. Jerome treated him with still less ceremony. He reproached him bitterly with not having answered his many letters. He reminded him that Christ had preached humility and given example of it; that pride had destroyed Satan and the Jewish people. Then in a tone half-jesting half-serious, he called upon him to write: "Here have I sent you ten letters, if I mistake not, full of good wishes and prayers; and you, you deign not to

---

15. *Epist.* 11.

reply, not so much as a *mu*. The Lord spoke to His servants! You will not speak to a brother. A truce to reproaches, say you. So be it; but, believe me, if I were not restrained by respect for my pen, I should make you pay so dear for the wrongs you have done that you would end by replying, if only through irritation. But if it is the nature of man to be irritated, it is the duty of a Christian to refrain from all insult. I return, then, to my manner of old. Once more I beg you to render me affection for affection; we serve the same Master; answer me. Greeting in the Lord."

Certainly that is an original way of demanding a reply to one's letters. Did the monk Antonius, this time, decide to write? We cannot be sure; such was the feeling against Jerome in the ascetical world of Hemona.

Another time it was the turn of his aunt Castorina. There was a long-standing quarrel between them. It pained him, and in his desert solitude he dreamed of reconciliation. To a first letter, now lost, the inflexible aunt had not replied. He returned to the charge, largely because of a scruple he felt as a Christian, unwilling to have upon his conscience the remorse for this family quarrel. He began with a batch of verses from Scripture on the forgiveness of insults and the mutual overlooking of wrong. Then he delivered a final ultimatum to Castorina. If she still refused the proffered reconciliation, he summoned her to the judgment seat of God, where she would be in evil case. "I beg

SAINT JEROME: THE EARLY YEARS

of you, as I did last year in another letter, that the peace the Lord has left us should be re-established between us. Let Christ consider my desire and your dispositions. Soon before His tribunal, reconciliation will have its reward and discord its punishment. If you refuse peace, which God forbid, it will not be my fault. The present letter, once read, will suffice to absolve me."[16] But Castorina was a woman to drag her rancour with her to the Last Judgment itself.

In his letters from the desert Jerome often spoke of Heliodorus, the companion ever-awaited, whose place was marked off in the cave![17] Following the promise made at the moment of their separation, he wrote some time after his arrival in the desert to give his impressions. To win over his friend he put into this letter his whole soul and all his eloquence, in a characteristic mingling of pathetic appeals, and friendly reproaches, arguments, familiar memories and sheer poetry.

Having recalled the grief he had felt at the time of Heliodorus' departure, Jerome summed up his impressions in a phrase: "I invite you to return; come in haste."[18] He recalled their conversations at Antioch. Heliodorus had alleged family reasons; Jerome replied with Scriptural texts, which commanded the true Christian to leave country

---

16. *Epist.* 13.
17. *Epist.* 5, 2; 6, 2; 9.
18. *Epist.* 14, 1.

PAUL MONCEAUX

and family to follow the Master. An ascetic was true to his undertaking—and ensured his salvation—only if he renounced the world completely.[19] Heliodorus had, it is true, urged his intention of becoming a priest. But nothing was harder than to achieve salvation as a priest, so formidable were the duties and responsibilities of the clergy.

As conclusion to these eloquent arguments, Jerome intoned his hymn to the desert—the desert of the hermits, where in solitude and peace one might find the way to Paradise. He sketched the portrait of the perfect anchorite, with his sufferings and his dignity.[20] He ended with a magnificent picture of the Last Judgment, the thought of which must dominate the present life: "The day will come whereon our body, now corruptible and mortal, will put on incorruption and immortality. Happy the servant whom the Lord shall find watching! Then, at the sound of the trumpet, the earth will tremble with its peoples, while you will rejoice. Before the Lord Judge, the world will cry piteously, and all the tribes of men will beat their breasts. Of those who were once most mighty kings will be seen the naked flanks heaving. There will be seen Venus with her son. Jove will appear with his thunderbolts,[21] and the fool Plato with

---

19. *Epist.* 14, 2–7.
20. *Epist.* 14, 10.
21. Instead of "Venus with her son...," Hilberg (in *Corpus Scriptorum ecclesiasticorum latinorum*) gives a different reading: *Exhibetur cum prole sua vere tunc ignitus Juppiter.*

SAINT JEROME: THE EARLY YEARS

his disciples. The arguments of Aristotle will avail nothing. Then you, poor and ignorant, will exult and laugh and say 'There is my crucified God, there is my Judge.'"[22]

Re-reading this letter later, Jerome accused himself of having sacrificed something to rhetoric.[23] He may not have been wrong. But neither were those admirers of Jerome wrong, who—like the repentant Fabiola—learned these pages by heart and sought in them a rule of life.[24] In spite of the flowers of rhetoric, the letter to Heliodorus is the finest panegyric, in the whole history of Christian asceticism, of the desert and the anchorite's life.

To this eulogy of the desert and its guests Jerome soon added a pendant—the eulogy of the first hermit.

---

22. *Epist.* 14, 11.
23. *Epist.* 52, 1.
24. *Epist.* 77, 9.

CHAPTER IV

THE *LIFE* OF SAINT PAUL THE HERMIT

CURIOUS by nature, with a taste for history, Jerome could not but be interested in the origins of this new way of life that he was following in the desert. He had long known the *Life of St. Anthony*, written in Greek by Athanasius of Alexandria and translated into Latin by his friend Evagrios of Antioch. Then, as now, St. Anthony was generally considered as the initiator of the hermit life. Yet in Egypt it was said that earlier still a certain Paul of Thebes had lived long in the desert, that Anthony had paid him homage as his master, that as to this there was the witness of Amathus and Macarius, two of Anthony's own disciples. Jerome had probably been told of these traditions by some of the Egyptians, bishops or monks, exiled in Syria, or else by the clerics who came from Alexandria to visit them. Fascinated by their stories, he thought he could cast a new light upon the origins of anchoritism. Hence the charming little work composed by him in the desert, probably in 376, entitled *Life of St. Paul, the first Hermit*. It was a sort of preface to the story of St. Anthony.

SAINT JEROME: THE EARLY YEARS

At the beginning Jerome, along with his sources, indicated the object of his work. Since there was no mention of Paul of Thebes either in the Greek biography of Anthony or in the Latin adaptation, the gap must be filled. He, Jerome, would give certain information about the youth of the first hermit and his end, but could say nothing of what lay between, as no one knew.[1]

Then came the story. It was during the persecutions of Decius or Valerian,[2] which raged violently in Egypt, that the vocation of the first of the hermits had declared itself. He had been born in the Lower Thebaïd. About the age of sixteen, he lost his parents. With his sister, who was already married, he had a rich heritage to share. He was a young man, very gentle, very pious, with a passion for Greek letters and the sciences of Egypt. When the persecution broke out he retired to a distant city, where he seemed to be safe. Unfortunately his brother-in-law was a rogue, a blackmailer with an eye on his fortune; to extort money this man threatened to denounce him to the persecutors.[3]

In this extremity Paul fled to certain mountain solitudes, where he found a safe retreat. Little by little his liking grew for these solitudes and he buried himself in them more and more completely. One day, at the foot of a rock,

---

1. *Vita Pauli primi eremitae*, 1 (Prologus).
2. Ibid., 2–3.
3. Ibid., 4.

he saw a cave closed by a stone. Removing the obstacle, he began to explore the interior. First he found a large vestibule open to the sky, shadowed by an ancient palm tree. A thread of clear water sprang up before the cave, filled a little natural basin, then ran away into the earth. The vestibule opened into subterranean chambers, formerly inhabited and still containing all the apparatus for coining money; this pleasant cave had been a haunt of counterfeiters.

There Paul of Thebes set up his abode. He took immense joy in it, "as in a dwelling presented him by God."[4] He lived there more than a century in solitude and prayer. He never wanted for anything, clothing himself in leaves from the palm, drinking the spring water, feeding on dates and a piece of bread brought him each day by a crow. That was all Jerome knew of his hero's life to the age of a hundred and twelve.

Paul was one hundred and thirteen when he was visited by St. Anthony. The latter was then a comparative youngster, only ninety years of age, and barely sixty-five years in the desert. In spite of this he had, three days before, had a movement of pride: he had said within himself that he was the most perfect of monks, dwelling in the most remote solitude. The following night he learnt by divine revelation that another monk, much more perfect, lived in a solitude

---

4. Ibid., 6.

SAINT JEROME: THE EARLY YEARS

still more remote. At the same time he received the command to pay a visit to this inimitable confrère.

At earliest dawn he took his staff and set out, going deeper and deeper into the desert, counting upon God to guide him. At midday, as he was trudging on under a blazing sun and still saw nothing, he told himself for his encouragement: "I have confidence in God; He will be able as he has promised, to show me his oldest servant." All at once he saw a strange being—half man, half horse. Prudently, fearing some trick of the Devil, he made a sign of the cross. Then he questioned the monster: "Eh, you, tell me where lives hereabouts the servant of God." The centaur tried to answer, by certain almost inarticulate sounds which were lost in the depths of an enormous beard. But with his right hand he pointed in the direction required, then galloped off out of sight.[5]

Somewhat startled, Anthony continued on his way. Further on, in a rocky valley, he saw approaching him a small man with a nose like an eagle's beak, horns on his forehead, and goat's feet. Once more he was on guard against the Devil. But the other, seeming harmless enough, made signs of friendship, offering dates and begging him in return to pray to the Saviour for him and his. Astonished to discover in this savage an adorer of Christ, Anthony shed

---

5. Ibid., 7.

tears of joy. Then he thought of the folly of the idolaters and thundered against them. While he was still speaking, the satyr had disappeared as swift as a bird.[6]

Yet Anthony marched on two days more. He now saw naught but the tracks of animals in the desert immensity. He passed the second night in prayer. The next day, in the half light of dawn, he saw a she-wolf panting with thirst; he followed her with his eyes to the foot of a mountain. There in his turn he went. He found himself standing before the entrance of a cave which was still deep in darkness. He ventured in, taking the shortest of steps, holding his breath, pausing, straining his ear for the slightest sound. Suddenly between the dark masses of rock he saw a light. In his joy he hurried his pace; but he kicked against a stone which rolled with a great noise. The noise of the stone was answered by other sounds in the depths of the cave—it was Paul of Thebes closing his door and pushing the bolt. For several hours, till the middle of the day, Anthony remained outside the door, begging the old hermit to open to him. At last Paul was reassured, or, at any rate, he changed his mind. The bolt was drawn and he appeared smiling. The two anchorites fell into each other's arms, calling each other by name like old friends.[7]

---

6. Ibid., 8.
7. Ibid., 9.

SAINT JEROME: THE EARLY YEARS

When they were seated the following conversation took place.

"Behold," said Paul, "here is the one you have sought with so much fatigue, a poor old man with mouldering limbs and an unkempt crop of white hair. It is still a man that you look upon, but it will soon be a little dust." Then the centenarian asked news of the world he had abandoned nearly a century before. Anthony replied as best he could, when a crow came and perched upon a branch, whence it descended with tiny wing-beats to lay a morsel of bread before the hermits. "Behold!" said Paul, "see how the Lord in His goodness, in His mercy, sends us our meal. These sixty years I have received each day the half of a loaf. Today for your coming Christ has doubled the ration."[8]

They sat at food outside the cave, beside the fountain. Then there was a contest of politeness between the two hermits, which should break the bread. To quench their thirst they had only to lean over the spring. The banquet over, they gave thanks to God. Already the desert was growing dark around them. They passed the night in holy vigil.

The next morning Paul said to Anthony: "Now is arrived the time of my last sleep.... You are sent by the Lord to bury my poor body, or rather to render earth to earth."[9]

---

8. Ibid., 10.
9. Ibid., 11.

Anthony burst into sobs, begging that he, too, might die. Paul continued: "No, your brethren still have need of you, who must form them by your example. Go then, I pray you; go find the mantle given you by Athanasius the bishop; bring it to cover my body." This, as the biographer remarks, was simply Paul's way of sparing his friend the sight of his death-agony. Anthony resigned himself. He took the road back to his hermitage, with a feverish haste that brought a touch of youth to his ninety-year-old legs.[10]

He arrived home deeply weary. Yet he did not linger. He entered his cell only to get the mantle. He started back at once, doubling his stages, fearing to find his master no longer living. He was approaching the cave, when he fell in ecstasy before a radiant vision; surrounded by a band of angels, in the midst of a choir of prophets and apostles, Paul was ascending into heaven in a great blaze of light. A sight no less moving awaited the traveller in the cave; kneeling, head erect, hands joined, the body of the saint was as though still in prayer.[11]

The moment had come for the fulfilment of his divine mission. Anthony wrapped the body in the mantle and bore it outside. While he sang the customary hymns and psalms he despaired of being able to proceed to the burial,

---

10. Ibid., 12.
11. Ibid., 13–15.

SAINT JEROME: THE EARLY YEARS

having no spade to dig. Suddenly, from the depths of the desert he saw two lions coming swiftly. The beasts went straight to the saint's body. First they stretched themselves at its feet, with mournful roaring. Then, tearing the soil with their paws, they hollowed out the grave. Their task accomplished, they approached Anthony and began to lick his hands and feet—with suppliant air, their heads lowered and their ears twitching, they seemed to await their reward. The hermit gave them his blessing, then dismissed them with a sign. When the lions were gone he took the body on his shoulders, placed it in the grave, flung the sand back upon it. His mission done, he thought he might take over the inheritance—the tunic Paul had fashioned for himself with interlaced palm leaves. This tunic Anthony carried off as the most precious of relics. Henceforth he never failed to wear it on the feasts of Easter and Pentecost.[12]

After the story, the moral. With the triumphant poverty of Paul of Thebes Jerome contrasted the miseries that wait upon the rich.[13] He ended with this prayer to the reader, sharpened into an epigram: "I conjure you, who read this work, remember Jerome the sinner. If the Lord gave him the choice, he would far rather have the tunic of Paul with his merits than the purple of kings with their torments."[14]

---

12. Ibid., 16.
13. Ibid., 17.
14. Ibid., 18.

PAUL MONCEAUX

That in outline is the story. It enchanted the literary public. But also it brought Jerome many critics. There were unpleasant people who denounced it as a mere rhetorical exercise, accusing the author of having invented the whole thing, hero included. Against these charges Jerome made many protests—in the Prologue to his *Life of St. Hilarion*, in his *Chronicle*, in several of his letters—where he deliberately associated the names of St. Paul and St. Anthony, insisting on the relations between them.[15] He was not always believed. Even in our own day certain scholars have brought the original accusation against him.

Certainly he is the first writer to mention St. Paul the Hermit, for the Greek *Lives* of his hero are later than his own and simply translate or adapt it. Hence the charge against his good faith. Yet Jerome indicated his sources, oral traditions of Egypt. That the legend held a large place in these traditions is beyond dispute. That Jerome's imagination embroidered upon it is not improbable. But the legend itself had probably taken its rise in historical facts, particularly as to the youth of the hero and his contact with St. Anthony. At any rate, we have proof that Paul of Thebes did really exist; as early as the end of the fourth century, he was the object of a cultus in Egypt, at Oxyrhyncus; this we

---

15. *Vita Hilarionis*, 1 (Prologus); *Chron. ad ann.* 356; *Epist.* 22, 36; 58, 5; 108, 6.

SAINT JEROME: THE EARLY YEARS

know from a document of the time, a petition addressed to the emperors Valentinian, Theodosius and Arcadius by the Luciferian priests Marcellinus and Faustinas.[16] Let us then take Jerome's story for what it is: a pleasant little edifying tale, a blending of legend with history, of the poetic and picturesque with reality.

Jerome has even been accused of lacking critical sense —because of the centaur, the satyr, the wolf, the crow, the lions! It is difficult to treat this seriously. Obviously every literary genre had then its own proper rules; and a storyteller—even were the story a saint's life—aimed above all at pleasing, and wrote down what he had heard as the most absolute matter of course. Jerome has proved in other fields that he had a sufficiently acute critical sense; but in this case he was handling popular traditions—poetic and quite harmless—to which the ordinary criteria of reason or faith had simply no application. Meeting one of those centaurs so often spoken of by his beloved poets, he spoke of it as they had done—asking only if it were a phantom sent by God or a monster born of the desert.[17] As to the satyr, for his own amusement he relates a curious anecdote in support of its existence: the story of a strange being, probably some great ape, which had recently been on exhibition at Alexandria;

---

16. On the historic reality of St. Paul of Thebes, see Delehaye, *C. R. de l'Académie des inscriptions* (1926), pp. 27–28.
17. *Vita Pauli*, 7.

on its death, the body had been salted, sent to Antioch and shown to the emperor.[18] It is sheer absurdity to take seriously these mythological phantoms; Jerome, a hagiographer for the nonce and still a rhetorician, was charmed to find them in a Christian tradition, which he set down with a smile.

A real personage in a poetic framework of legend: it was precisely this combination that attracted Jerome in the first place, and set the note for his story. Popular imagination had brought a centaur, a satyr, a she-wolf across St. Anthony's path, and had given St. Paul the crow to fetch his bread and the lions to dig his grave. St. Jerome never dreamt of suppressing all this phantasmagoria; he simply made the best use of it. This time, he tells us, he aimed at a popular style, to be understood by all. He feared, even then, that he had not always succeeded in this, and he excused himself neatly: "Fill a bottle with water; it still retains the perfume with which it was impregnated when it was new."[19] And indeed there still lingers in his work a perfume of the rhetoric he had not yet shed. For all that, the story is of the popular sort. It moves in an atmosphere of fairy-tale, in a marvellous region where nature is dominated by the supernatural, monsters rub shoulders with

---

18. Ibid., 8.
19. *Epist.* 10, 3.

SAINT JEROME: THE EARLY YEARS

real beings, the beasts are in the service of the man protected by God.

The work had a great success. It was much read in Rome, where it made its author's name. It was appreciated in the East, as the two Greek versions—one a translation, the other an adaptation—testify. It even helped to draw certain unquiet imaginations towards asceticism. Further, it opened the way to the hagiographical literature of the coming centuries—a literature almost entirely legendary and imaginative; very different from the accounts of the martyrs in the early centuries. Finally, and fortunately, it inspired many works of art and one masterpiece.

Here I speak only of the masterpiece which, by an ingenious arrangement, assembles on one canvas practically all the scenes of the story. I mean, of course, Velazquez' famous picture in the Prado at Madrid: *The Visit of St. Anthony to St. Paul the Hermit*. The two men, both bearded and bald, both simple in their majesty, are seated at the edge of a picturesque valley near a spring, beneath a great tree, at the entrance of a cave which runs away to the right under an enormous rock. The centenarian, part naked, emaciated, splendid in spite of all his rags, is announcing his approaching end, raising to heaven his dazzled eyes and his clasped hands. St. Anthony, in an abbot's dress of sombre colours, listens with sorrowful surprise, seeming to repel the prediction with anxious look and hands moving feverishly. Everything in the scene—expression of face, attitudes, gestures, landscape—is imposing in its grandeur. Nothing mars the harmony; not even the episodes in the background, drawn likewise from St. Jerome's story. In the right background is the arrival of the visitor, knocking at the door of the cell. Near the top of the rock, the crow descending with the loaf of bread. To the left, lower down the valley, the preparations for the burial—St. Anthony kneeling near the lifeless body of his master, the two lions digging the sand with their paws to prepare the grave. All that is picturesque and poetic in Jerome's story has passed into Velazquez' picture.

CHAPTER V

THE "TEMPTATIONS" OF ST. JEROME

The hermit life so long dreamed of and now realised, a life vowed to prayer and study, was at first all bathed in light from heaven. In the early months he went from rapture to rapture. The colony of hermits around him seemed like another Choir of the Blessed.

The enchantment was over soon enough. Little by little natural objects and nature herself took on another colour. He had hours of anguish, days and nights of suffering. He had to struggle against illness, loneliness, memories of the world, carnal passions. His body, which had always been delicate and which now he treated so ill, rebelled against his long fasts and the excesses of his austerity.[1] Solitude, since it gave him too much to himself, became a source of suffering. The desert of which but now he had spoken as a poet or a painter, had become a place of desolation, a furnace, a prison even. In his moments of acutest anguish he took a horror for his very cave, the partner in his guilty

---

1. *Epist.* 6; 17, 3.

thoughts.[2] In vain he sought to master himself, redoubling his fasts, kneeling before a crucifix, humbling himself and weeping, asking pardon. Even in his cell, before Christ crucified, he felt the Devil within him. Then he would rush out alone into the desert, into the night, hoping to escape from himself, seeking God in the heavens, crying out his faults, imploring forgiveness.

The frightful torment of the sufferings of that time breaks out, flames out, in the dramatic account he gives of his temptations:

> Oh, how often in the desert, in that desolate solitude, burnt dry by the heat of the sun, a forbidding habitation for monks, I fancied I was back again amidst the delights of Rome. I sat alone, for I was filled with bitterness. Shapeless in a sack, I loathed my own body.... Daily I wept, daily I groaned. If sometimes the sleep I fought against overcame me, my bones scarcely hanging together, drove into each other as I lay naked on the earth.... I, then, who for fear of hell had condemned myself to such a prison, I the companion only of scorpions and wild beasts, often fancied that I was amidst bands of girls. My face was pale with fasting, but in my

---

2. *Epist.* 15, 2; 16, 2; 17, 2–3; 22, 7.

SAINT JEROME: THE EARLY YEARS

> numbed body my mind was fevered with desires; in my flesh dead before death, only the fires of lust raged on. Destitute of all help I cast myself at the feet of Jesus, watered them with my tears, dried them with my hair. My rebellious flesh I tried to conquer by weeks of fasting.... I remember that often times I cried out the day and night together, and I ceased not to beat my breast till a rebuke from the Lord bought me back to peace. My very cell I feared for its share in my thoughts. Enraged with myself, I rushed alone deep into the desert. All that I saw there, the depths of the valleys, rugged mountains, cliffs and crags, became the place of my prayer, the dungeon of my unhappy flesh.[3]

Never has any man painted more powerfully the tortures of a soul at war with its body, at war with itself.

This description, admired by all writers, has had an extraordinary place in the history of art. The typical figure that emerges from it has had so great a fascination for artists, that the works still existent are to be counted by hundreds; scarcely a gallery that does not contain one. As St. Jerome had become the patron of clerics and of many congregations, it was common for churches and convents to

---

3. *Epist.* 22, 7.

have scenes of his life done in pictures or bas-reliefs; favourite among such scenes was this of the temptations, which, with its unique combination of devotion, moral lesson and sheer picturesqueness, spoke at once to faith, to reason and to the imagination.

St. Jerome's temptations naturally recall St. Anthony's. But the artistic conception is very different. In their Temptations of St. Anthony, artists, inspired by the fantastic descriptions in the Greek life, have shown the saint at grips with the Devil, with demons and monsters of every sort, even with women. Jerome's account has ordinarily set imaginations working in a totally different direction. There are no women here, no monsters, no devils. The drama is always within the soul—the remorse of a sinner punishing himself. We have seen what he said: "Destitute of all help, I cast myself at the feet of Jesus.... I cried out the day and night together, and I ceased not to beat my breast...."[4] In such phrases is the origin of the typical figure of St. Jerome, kneeling before a crucifix, beating his breast with a stone. Variants are rare, seldom going beyond secondary details, of landscape or accessories. I need not add that in most of the pictures we find the same two anachronisms—the transformation of the young hermit into an aged man, and the premature presence of the lion.

---

4. *Epist.* 22, 7.

SAINT JEROME: THE EARLY YEARS

This type of *Jerome Penitent*, which appears towards the end of the fourteenth century, at once became so popular that it imposed itself upon all artists and remained practically unaltered till the eighteenth century. Certain painters, like Ribera, have treated the subject many times with no notable modifications. This persistence of one type is in no way surprising: it is accounted for by the demands of a clientèle of priests and monks, obstinately attached to a tradition. Consider two examples out of a great number.

First, a Titian, in the Louvre—of which there are replicas at the Brera in Milan, at Turin and elsewhere. In the foreground of a rugged and desolate landscape, with a few gleams of light shining through, Jerome, grey-haired and grey-bearded, kneels before a great pine, his chest bare. In his right hand is the stone with which he is about to strike his breast. He has his eye fixed, his head and his whole body tensely drawn, towards a great crucifix, half-seen on a dark background of rocks.

But the greatest of all these pictures is a sketch by Leonardo da Vinci, a cameo in the Vatican. At the entrance of a cave, before a sombre wall of rocks made more sombre still by contrast with luminous perspectives far off, Jerome is kneeling on his left knee. He is almost naked, though a drapery hangs from his left shoulder to the ground. He is bald, fleshless, the bones showing through the ghastly emaciation of the body. His right arm is tense to strike, and in his hand is a stone. The gesture and attitude, the expression of face, the head bending under the weight of remorse, the eye, with its double brilliance of fever and faith in God, in its socket fretted with tears—all betrays a measureless anguish. The lion, on the ground before him, looks at his master and seems to share his agony. And in that desolate landscape nature is at one with the misery of man.

The countless pictures of *Jerome Penitent* have their counterpart in another group of pictures showing him consoled and almost triumphant. Oddly enough, these, too, have their source—or one of their sources—in his description of the Temptations. At the time of those anguished flights into the desert Jerome often returned, restored to peace and, as it were, transfigured by a heavenly vision. "I call the Lord to witness," he says, "after much weeping, after much gazing upward to heaven, I sometimes seemed to be among choirs of angels; and in joy and gladness I sang: *Post te in odorem unguentorum tuorum currimus*."[5] From this come two groups of pictures. In the one, angels appear to Jerome. In the other, as in his posthumous appearances to different persons, he is actually mingling with the heavenly choirs.

Among these supernatural representations the most curious are those which treat of the summons to the Last

---

5. *Epist.* 22, 7 (verse from Cant. of Cant. 1:3).

SAINT JEROME: THE EARLY YEARS

Judgment. Jerome was at that time haunted by the end of the world, as is shown by those letters from the desert in which he appealed to the Judgment throne of Christ against the accusations of his enemies.[6] Particularly was his imagination possessed by the trumpet before whose note all things were to fall away. "Lo," he cried, "the trumpet sounds from heaven, and in the clouds comes the Lord armed, to overcome the world...."[7] Then at the voice of the trumpet the earth will tremble with its peoples. Before the Lord Judge the world will cry piteously, and all the tribes of men will beat their breasts."[8] Jerome had meditated so much on this trumpet, that he finished by hearing it—especially at night, when it woke him with a start.

Such is the scene which has attracted so many painters, who have found material for their pictures in his letters as well as in his account of the Temptations. The subject recurs, with certain variations, in paintings by Annibal Carrache, Ribera and Gessi in Naples, Ribera again and Antonio Pereda in Madrid. A Guercino in the Louvre, *The Vision of St. Jerome*, shows him, with a movement of terror, raising his right arm towards an angel who, from a stormy sky, is sounding the trumpet. Sigalon, in a picture once famous, takes up the same theme with additions: lying on

---

6. *Epist.* 6; 11; 13., cf. *Epist.* 14, 3 and 11.
7. *Epist.* 14, 2.
8. *Epist.* 14, 11.

a rock, with the sleeping lion, an open book and a skull nearby, Jerome wakes, terror-stricken, raising his right arm towards three angels, of whom two are sounding the trumpets of the Last Judgment, while the third points him to heaven. Here the Calvary of Jerome Penitent becomes his apotheosis.

CHAPTER VI

WARFARE IN THE DESERT

JEROME'S worst sufferings in the desert did not come from illness, nor from solitude, nor from remorse; they did not even come from the Devil—at least not directly. They came from theology: the quarrelsome theology of his neighbours, hermits or other monks. For these quarrels there were two reasons, or pretexts: the schism of Antioch and the controversy on the hypostases.

Even to the desert, writes our young hermit, "the Enemy has obstinately pursued me, so that now, in solitude, I have to suffer wars still more terrible. On one side rages the frenzy of the Arians, supported by the powers of the world. On the other are the three factions of a Church cloven by schism, which seek to draw me to themselves. And against me is ranged the ancient authority of the monks of the neighbourhood."[1]

When Jerome left Antioch the town had already three rival bishops: Meletius, the elect of the majority, under

---

1. *Epist.* 16, 2.

suspicion of sympathy with Arianism; Euzoios, chosen by the Arians; Paulinus, chosen by the intransigent Catholics. From 376 the town had a fourth bishop: Vitalis, ordained by Apollinaris of Laodicea. Each of these four bishops had his partisans among the monks of the desert, who discussed among themselves the merits of their respective leaders, with sharp exchange of syllogisms, and insults, and occasionally blows.

More potent even than the fourfold schism, theology was setting hearts on fire in the waste places of Syria. The controversy on the hypostases was at its height, rousing Christian circles in the East to frenzy. From the councils it had spread to the crowds; and the echo resounded in the very depths of the deserts.

One single *ousia* or divine substance, in three *hypostases* or persons: such was the formula adopted by Meletius and the majority of Orientals to express the Catholic teaching on the Trinity. Unfortunately the word *hypostasis* was liable to a double interpretation. Following its etymology, it had originally signified "substance," and for many it retained this meaning. As the faith of the simple was confused by this, sectarian passion exploited the confusion to the full. The party of Paulinus, who held to the primitive sense and spoke of one single hypostasis, made accusation of Arianism against the party of Meletius and these retorted with an accusation of Sabellianism. In spite of the

SAINT JEROME: THE EARLY YEARS

decisions of the Council authorising the profession of either one hypostasis or three according to the old or new sense of the word, the partisans of Meletius and Paulinus stigmatised each other as heretics. They were at one only in hurling anathemas against the Arianism of Euzoios and the heretical Christology of Vitalis.

These bitter controversies, wherein theological differences were complicated by the rivalry of Churches, grew still more embittered in the gatherings of the monks of the desert—ascetics ardent of faith, their imagination overwrought in the long hours of their leisure by concentration on one idea, by fasting, by meditation. Living only for the hope of salvation, they were equally bent on the salvation of their neighbour. They made it their business to be sure that he was in the right way, so they asked him to explain his position, and they grew warm in argument to the point of frenzy. From time to time, Christian charity for the moment taking fresh hold, they made sincere efforts at mutual understanding. But the harder they tried to agree, the more vigorously disagreement blazed up. And charity suffered shipwreck in the mystery of the hypostases; and the Church of Antioch was rent more deeply than ever by the schism of its four bishops.

Into these quarrels Jerome was drawn in his own despite. They were oddly interested in his salvation in that Graeco-Syrian world where a Latin, uprooted from his own land, was easily seen as an intruder, an object of suspicion. It was all very well for him to shut himself up in his cell, to hide in the desert; they knocked at his door, followed him into the sands or the rocks, to ask him what he thought on the hypostases. Everyone wanted to enlist him in his own party. And each party could bring some sort of pressure to bear on him. The Meletians, for instance, had the argument of numbers—since their Church contained by far the most members. For the Arianisers, there was the support of the civil authorities, the Emperor Valens favouring Arianism. The followers of Paulinus naturally appealed to the relations he had had with Paulinus at Antioch, and his close friendship with the priest Evagrios. The Vitalis party could remind him that he had followed the lectures of Apollinaris their chief. Of this quadruple propaganda, the most formidable and the most pertinacious was that of the Meletians; their insistence was all the greater because Jerome was particularly suspect by reason of his previous relations with the Paulinus party.

We may imagine his embarrassment. At Antioch he had seen much of Paulinus, because Paulinus, the protégé of Pope Damasus, was the bishop of his host Evagrios. As quarrels among the Easterns did not interest him, he had not been much affected by the schism. Once in the desert he had the shock of discovering, through the statements of the monks his neighbours, that the partisans both of

SAINT JEROME: THE EARLY YEARS

Meletius and Vitalis made equal claim with Paulinus to communion with the Roman Church. "It was in vain," as he wrote to Pope Damasus "that I cried: 'If anyone is united with the chair of Peter he is with me.' Meletius, Vitalis and Paulinus alike declared themselves in communion with you. I could believe it, if only one of them affirmed it; but either two are lying, or all three."[2]

Thus in doubt, Jerome had resolved to remain neutral among the parties in conflict over the bishopric of Antioch. For his religious duties he betook himself to certain Egyptian bishops in the district, who had been sent to Syria as exiles, and whom he knew to be in communion with Pope Damasus.[3] It was a neat solution, permitting him to be rid—without committing himself—of all those over-zealous souls who came to urge their bishop's claims.

But theology continued to lay siege to his cave. The Meletians in particular made a point of assuring themselves that he admitted the three hypostases. But, he could only recognise one since, like Paulinus of Antioch, like Evagrios, like the Churches of Alexandria and Rome, he remained faithful to the word's primitive meaning of "substance." To prevent misconstruction he made it his absolute rule, in his professions of faith, not to use the Greek term *hypostasis*

---

2. *Epist.* 16, 2.
3. *Epist.* 15, 2.

at all. That was precisely where his worst troubles arose; for his visitors—and inquisitors—were passionately set upon the word itself, seeing in it a test of orthodoxy. "Three hypostases," he wrote, "such is the new formula that these sons of Arians, these Provincials, claim to impose upon *me*, a Roman… We ask what, according to them, one must understand by three hypostases: 'Three subsistent persons,' they affirm. We reply that such is our faith. But the meaning is not enough for them; they must have the word itself; some spell is hidden in its syllables. In vain do we cry: 'If anyone does not confess three hypostases in the sense of three subsistent persons, let him be anathema!' Because we do not use the same words, we are called heretics."[4]

What aggravated the double misconstruction was Jerome's temper and his caustic wit.

Challenged to pronounce as to the hypostases and as to the legitimacy of the rival claimants to the see of Antioch, he tried to remain neutral, as was his right. But he declared too roundly that local quarrels were no affair of his, as a Christian of Rome. By this disdainful attitude he displeased all parties and ran some danger of drawing the fire of them all. A poor hand at diplomacy, with a touch of brutality in his candour, he had not the art to evade the issue politely—he grew irritated, discussed matters in a tone

---

4. *Epist.* 15, 3.

SAINT JEROME: THE EARLY YEARS

of irony, poked fun at over-inquisitive visitors, dismissed them too brusquely. He ended by having all the monks of the district up in arms against him.

One day it occurred to him as a way out to write to *his* bishop, Pope Damasus, whom he may have known, or at any rate seen, in Rome. He wished to consult him both upon the schism and upon the hypostases, upon the question of fact and the question of doctrine. To steer a right course, as he said, among the dissensions and doctrinal errors of the East, he thought it his duty to interrogate the Roman Church, which preserved the apostolic tradition and to which he belonged by his baptism.[5] A voluntary exile in the Syrian desert, he wished to remain in communion with Rome. For that reason he had so far refrained from joining any of the bishops who were disputing the see of Antioch. He declared bluntly: *Non novi Vitalem, Meletium respus, ignoro Paulinum.*[6] Easterns suspect of heresy were claiming to impose upon him their belief in three hypostases; playing on the double meaning of the word, they even accused him of heresy.[7] Yet he thought that one must be bound by the definitions of the Council of Nicaea: one hypostasis or divine substance in three persons.[8] He

---

5. *Epist.* 15, 1.
6. *Epist.* 15, 2.
7. *Epist.* 15, 3.
8. *Epist.* 15, 4.

conjured the pope to tell him if one must accept or not the new doctrine of the three hypostases, and to inform him with which of the three bishops of Antioch—all three self-styled Catholics—one must be in communion.[9] The letter sent off, Jerome lived for the reply. He had hoped it would be prompt. He waited months, perhaps a year. He was still waiting, when he decided to write again. This time he consulted the pope only on the schism at Antioch; and this, after all, was sufficient, since the question of who was bishop implicated the question of doctrine. He apologised for his insistence upon a reply, justifying his importunity by examples borrowed from Scripture.[10] He reminded the pope that he was one of his faithful, baptised in Rome, now a hermit in the Syrian desert. In these solitudes, where he, alas, had not found peace, he had to defend himself at the same time against the Arians, who had the backing of the civil authorities, and against the partisans of the three self-styled Catholic bishops of Antioch, who were all worrying him to enlist in their factions. In principle he was for whichever of the three bishops could be proved to be in communion with the inheritor of the chair of St. Peter; but all three made much of their relations with the Roman Church. He begged the pope, then, to indicate to him the

---

9. *Epist.* 15, 5.
10. *Epist.* 16, 1.

SAINT JEROME: THE EARLY YEARS

one with whom it was his duty to be in communion. He finished with the touching phrase: "Do not despise a soul for which Christ died."[11]

In spite of this eloquent adjuration, everything suggests that the pope still did not reply; which is scarcely matter for surprise, if one grasps the circumstances and the diplomatic prudence of the Roman chancellery.

In appearance, Jerome was simply asking the Pope to lay down a line of conduct for him. In reality he knew very well, through his friends in Antioch, that Rome supported Paulinus and taught one hypostasis, in the sense of substance. Therefore, since he knew the answer in advance, he was merely seeking to shelter behind the authority of the Roman Church. He hoped to bring it to a categorical pronouncement, even to condemn Meletius and his three hypostases.

That precisely is why no answer came. Obviously, at Rome, there could be naught but approval for Jerome's Roman views on the two questions. But Pope Damasus could not then maintain these views without reservation, since the discussion between Rome and Antioch was still open. Now Jerome's letters showed clearly enough that in his overexcited state, he would never keep the answer to himself: in satisfying this young and ebullient hermit of the

---

11. *Epist.* 16, 2.

Syrian desert they would have risked envenoming relations with the East. Knowing that in the heat of the controversies an indiscreet use would have been made of his reply, the Pope feared to compromise the Church of Rome before the questions had been decided by the councils, and so perhaps provoke a rupture with the metropolitan Church of Antioch. Roman diplomacy avoided the risk by turning a deaf ear.

While Jerome was awaiting the Pope's reply to use it as weapon against his adversaries, the situation grew more acute in the desert of Chalcis, with its boiling religious passions. From discussions they passed to challenges, from challenges to insults, from insults to blows. More and more the colony of hermits was enveloped in an atmosphere of battle.

CHAPTER VII

FAREWELL TO THE DESSERT

EXASPERATED by these ceaseless quarrels, embittered by strife, sick in body and soul, ravaged by fever—and by anger—Jerome was in fear of still darker days to come. He saw the ring of hostile fellow-hermits closing in about him. The handful of reasonable monks with whom he had made alliance, persecuted like him by the fury of theologians, had gone off one by one, preferring, as they said, the society of wild beasts to that of such Christians.[1] He began to think of leaving a desert so clamorous, so saturated with hatred.

One winter's day, sick as usual, he received an unexpected letter, lecturing him in a kindly way, in the tone of one standing outside and above the quarrel. It was from a priest he knew, one Marcus, who probably served the hermits' church and who was anxious to restore peace; he asked Jerome to send him a profession of faith on the Trinity, which would, he hoped, calm and satisfy his adversaries.[2]

---

1. *Epist.* 17, 3.
2. *Epist.* 17, 4.

PAUL MONCEAUX

This friendly letter, inspired in an excellent man by Christian charity and the duties of his office, had upon Jerome's mind the effect of a wasp-sting on an open wound. It revived his sufferings, brought back to mind the long series of his disillusions, inflamed his resentment. He replied to Marcus' request by a vengeful diatribe against his persecutors and announced his immediate departure.

In this letter, written spiritedly on a note of invective, he began by declaring that he had meant to keep silence, but that out of regard to Marcus he had resolved to speak.[3] Particularly he wished to deal faithfully with the demoniac monks who surrounded him. He applied to them the lines of Virgil:

...quod genus hoc hominum?
quaeve hunc tam barbaramorem permittit patria?
hospitio prohibemur harenae, bella cient,
primaque vetant consistere tetra.[4]

And by way of justification for this classical allusion, he adds: "If I have made this quotation from a pagan poet, it is

---

3. *Epist.* 17, 1.
4. What men, what monsters, what inhuman race,
   What laws, what barb'rous customs of the place,
   Shut up a desert shore to drowning men,
   And drive us to the cruel seas again?
   (*Aeneid*, I, 539–541, translated by John Dryden)

SAINT JEROME: THE EARLY YEARS

that men who do not observe the peace of Christ should at least learn from a pagan to respect peace."[5]

What was the charge against him? That he was a heretic, a Sabellian—he whose faith was one with that of Pope Damasus and the Bishop of Alexandria. Anyhow, what business was it of these monks of the desert? He derided their pretensions and their pride: "I am ashamed to say it; from the caverns of our cells we damn the world. Under sackcloth and ashes we pass judgment on bishops. What means this regal pride under the tunic of a penitent?" He demanded of these turbulent souls that they leave him in peace. "Permit me, I pray, not to speak. Why do you send a man who deserves no hatred? I am a heretic, you say. What is that to you? Hold your peace, as you have already been told."[6] He had done no wrong to any man; he owed nothing to any man, since he lived by his labour. Why then these persecutions, these summonses, wherewith they harassed him with such obvious bad faith? "They do not want to leave me a corner of the desert. Every day they come to ask an account of my faith, as if I had been regenerated without making a profession of faith. I profess what they will; they are not content. I sign; they do not believe me."

---

5. *Epist.* 17, 2.
6. *Epist.* 17, 2.

What in reality was the reason of these persecutions? That they had sworn to make him go. Very well then; a little patience; he would go soon—the moment that the season and his health allowed it—even sooner, if necessary. "One thing alone they want," he cried, "that I should go from here. Very well, I am going. Already they have torn from me a part of my soul, my best-loved brethren: these desire to depart, *do* depart, declaring that it is better to dwell in the midst of wild beasts than with such Christians. As for me, if illness and the rigours of winter had not detained me, I should already have fled. Let them be patient till the coming of spring. I ask that the hospitality of the desert be granted me for a few months more. If even that delay appears too long, so be it! I go; to the Lord belongs the earth in its fullness. Let my persecutors be the only ones to ascend to heaven; for them alone be Christ dead; let them seize upon Him, possess Him, glory in Him. For me, God forbid that I should glory save in the cross of our Lord Jesus Christ."[7] As for the profession of faith that was asked for, Jerome declared that he had sent it in writing to St. Cyril (probably the Bishop of Chalcis). Beyond that, he called upon Marcus himself as witness of his orthodoxy.[8]

---

7. *Epist.* 17, 3.
8. *Epist.* 17, 4.

SAINT JEROME: THE EARLY YEARS

This stinging retort was like his last confession as a hermit: a confession vengeful, bitter, despairing; a strange contrast to that enthusiastic hymn with which he had hailed the desert two years before. The experiment was over. As he had announced to Marcus, the young hermit left his cave and the desert of Chalcis almost at once. It was probably about the early spring of 378 that he bade farewell to these over-peopled solitudes, where he had sought the road to Paradise and had not even found peace.

CHAPTER VIII

JEROME AT THIRTY

At the time when he made once more for Antioch, in flight from the monks of the desert and their aggressive theology, Jerome was about thirty. He was in the prime of talent as of age. Since his coming into Syria he had completed the first stage of his education—literature and rhetoric—by the technical education necessary for scholarship: learning Greek and Hebrew, instructing himself in the doctrines, the exegesis and the methods of Origen, arming for the future and for the service of the Church. Already known for his letters, he had just published a small masterpiece, the *Life* of St. Paul the Hermit. Before bringing to light the scholar dormant within him he had shown his power as letter-writer, satirist, narrator. Even so early, those rare gifts were in evidence which were to make him a master of style.

Peace the hermit had not found in his desert, but what was not in his mind, literary glory. And justly. His prose style as letter-writer, narrator, pamphleteer, is an enchantment. It is in structure almost classical; yet in it is some unnameable quality, more personal and vibrant, a verve and

SAINT JEROME: THE EARLY YEARS

freshness, a fancifulness, sudden popular touches, flashes of genius.

This talent as writer was in part bound up with the character of the man. With all his qualities and his virtues, Jerome had certain defects. His generous aspirations towards the ideal did not prevent his keeping a restless eye on what passed upon earth. With his friends he was kindness itself, but not always with others. Ardent and passionate, imaginative, with the eye of a satirist, emotional and impulsive, he was very stormy, sensitive, quick to anger, resentful, capable even of terrible bursts of violence, all of which brought to *him* many enemies, to his readers a feast of superb retorts. He had an immeasurable wit, mordant, sometimes malignant. Even to gain Paradise he would have found it hard to choke back a good jest.

These defects of character varied in quality according to the state of his health. Now Jerome was one of those men who always treated his body without the faintest consideration; and such men do not always die young. Already many times he had seen death close: at Antioch, then in the desert. More and more, illnesses were to wage war upon him, slowly undermining all his organs. In spite of everything he resisted ill-health for more than forty years; but his opponents paid for it.

A sick man and an irascible, with a heart of gold, but unquiet in mind and biting of tongue, a mighty warrior with the soul of an apostle, an unwearied student, a fresh and original writer: such was Jerome at thirty, when he turned his back on the monks of the desert to re-enter the world and face the unknown future.

Designed by Fiona Cecile Clarke, the Cluny Media *logo depicts a monk at work in the scriptorium, with a cat sitting at his feet.*

The monk represents our mission to emulate the invaluable contributions of the monks of Cluny in preserving the libraries of the West, our strivings to know and love the truth.

The cat at the monk's feet is Pangur Bán, from the eponymous Irish poem of the 9th century. The anonymous poet compares his scholarly pursuit of truth with the cat's happy hunting of mice. The depiction of Pangur Bán is an homage to the work of the monks of Irish monasteries and a sign of the joy we at Cluny take in our trade.

"Messe ocus Pangur Bán,
cechtar nathar fria saindan:
bíth a menmasam fri seilgg,
mu memna céin im saincheirdd."

www.ingramcontent.com/pod-product-compliance
Lightning Source LLC
Chambersburg PA
CBHW052140070526
44585CB00017B/1909